DROPSHIPPING
HOW TO PLAN YOUR ONLINE BUSINESS

By Dario Gallione

Copyright © Dario Gallione

All rights reserved including the right of reproduction in whole or in part in any form.

Sommario

INTRODUCTION 6
WHAT IS DROPSHIPPING? 11
    What is Dropship? 11
    How does Dropship work? 12
    What is OpenDropship? 12
BENEFITS OF DROPSHIPPING 15
REASONS TO CONSIDER DROP SHIPPING 17
PROS AND CONS OF DROPSHIPPING 21
    PROS OF DROPSHIPPING 21
    CONS OF DROPSHIPPING 23
DROPSHIPPING MYTHS 26
FACTS ABOUT DROPSHIPPING 31
WHO AND WHO SHOULDN'T VENTURE INTO DROPSHIPPING? 39
    Who is Dropshipping For? 39
    Who Isn't Drop Shipping For? 41
HOW TO START A DROPSHIPPING BUSINESS 44
    Identify a Market 44
STEPS TO BUILDING A SUCCESSFUL ONLINE DROP SHIPPING BUSINESS 48
DROPSHIPPING SUPPLIERS 55
    How to Find the Best Drop Shipping Suppliers 56
    Create your own online storefront 56
HOW TO SETUP A DROPSHIPPING STORE/WEBSITE 75
    Why Create a Dropshipping Website? 75

How to Set Up a Dropshipping Website in 4 Steps? 77

Where to Get Dropshipping Website Templates/Designs? ... 84

Must Have Dropshipping Plugins 86

Examples of Dropshipping Websites 88

The Best Dropshipping Partners/Companies to Work With. . 89

STRATEGIES TO PROMOTE YOUR DROPSHIPPING STORE 93

DROPSHIPPING MISTAKES THAT CAN DESTROY YOUR BUSINESS 100

HOW TO PROVIDE EXCEPTIONAL CUSTOMER SUPPORT IN DROPSHIPPING/SATISFYING YOUR CUSTOMERS 115

Essential skills to improve your customer service 122

Why good service improves the customer experience 131

How to handle tricky customer service scenarios 136

Customer satisfaction 138

Customer Effort Score 139

DROPSHIPPING TIPS 141

1. Educate Yourself Will Help A Lot 141

2. Know Your Niche More than Your Customers 142

3. Find the Right Supplier is Extremely Important 143

4. Automate Will Help Save Tons of Time 144

5. Conduct Competitive Intelligence Will Make Your Business Much Easier 145

6. Rev Up Your Customer Service Will Keep Your Customers Coming Back 147

7. Plan for Returns and Other Issues 148

8. Test your Product is Extremely Important 149

9. Put Effort into Your Website's Experience 150

10. Create Custom Product Images 151

11. Evaluate Profit Margin Will Earn You Much More 152

12. Featured Product Will Increase Your Sales 152

13. Focus on Marketing Will Drive You More Traffic 153

14. Know Your Customers Than Your Girlfriend 154

15. Learn From Mistakes Will Help You Grow Up 154

IMPORTANCE OF CONVERSION IN DROPSHIPPING 157

HOW TO RETAIN CUSTOMERS 162

MOST COMMON DROP SHIPPING PROBLEMS 176

Conclusion 183

INTRODUCTION

The whole spectrum of doing business has undergone a world of change in the last few decades. One of the latest online business ideas is dropship services. This online business involves a process in which manufacturers or suppliers deliver the products directly to the customers of the dropship business without the business having to pre-purchase or stock the goods. The best part of the bargain is that the business owner, or reseller, does not have to do any hard work such as inventing, designing, buying or making the product, testing the market, describing the product on the website, making the website attractive, or promoting the product.

The dropship services business owner just has to list the products on eBay and get orders for the products by using its own or the supplying company's descriptions and graphics. When the orders are received, the reseller supplies the information regarding the buyers' names and addresses and other details of the order, so that the supplier can send the products to the buyer. The company also collects the payment.

The business of dropship services can reap rich returns for the business owner, but the most important dropshipping guide is that it is necessary to take care of the business and customers to ensure that any buyers' complaints regarding poor product quality or delays between receipt of payments and delivery of goods are tended to promptly. Any negligence in providing necessary after-sales services and attending to complaints can tarnish the image of the company and lead to loss of revenue and future orders. In order to find an answer to how to dropship and how to start a dropshipping business, it is vital to select a reliable supplier. The wrong selection can have disastrous results. Follow the following steps before starting this type of business.

The first step for starting a dropship services business is that the sourcing of the suppliers should be done with great care. Simply select the suppliers recommended by other people. It is possible to get free or paid-for lists of dropshipping companies on Internet directory sites. Some give accurate information whereas others might be owned by unscrupulous suppliers, so avoid those particular recommendations.

Once a selection is made based on reliable recommendations, and after checking that the range of products that the business intends to deal are sold by the supplier, check the contact details provided by the supplier. Pertinent contact information such as phone number, email address, and a mailing address should be available on the supplier's website. Avoid any supplier with incorrect or with no contact information at all. Make sure the phone is answered and see how long it takes for the supplier to answer emails, which may come in handy later if you have a reason to contact them with a problem.

Since there can be disputes with the supplier regarding faulty goods or undelivered items, business terms and conditions of the supplier should be properly stated and understood by the reseller. Realize that the responsibilities of the business as a reseller are different than the responsibilities that the supplier would have toward the reseller.

As a reseller, the dropship services business has to pay resellers registration fees and, in some cases, ongoing subscription charges for the right to access the supplier's catalogue. Access for a limited time is normally allowed before registration. Before registering with any supplier, check whether it charges ongoing subscription fees. Fine print should also be checked well for any between-the-lines clauses.

Check whether the potential supplier holds enough stock of the products and they are not a middleman posing as a supplier. These middlemen place orders with the real supplier and when they receive orders from the reseller and, in this process, long delays can take place. These delays can result in losses to the customer and subsequent losses to the reseller because the payment would have to be refunded.

Find out how the supplier expects to receive payments because the most convenient mode would be the same by which the customer pays the reseller. This will save charges and time. It is also advisable to avoid having to pay by Wire Transfer or Telegraph Transfer because the risk is higher if there is no customer protection.

While choosing a supplier, avoid those sites that offer branded goods such as designer clothing and electrical goods at unbelievably low prices. Such low priced, so-called designer goods are bound to be fake unless the supplier is trustworthy and renowned and he has obtained the goods from a close-out, or if the goods are refurbished or Grade A returns. If the reseller sells fake goods, he can be accused of selling counterfeit goods.

Teaming up with artists and craftsmen for their creative products is a unique way to do dropship services business. These creative people usually lack marketing savvy. Visits to local craft fairs can provide unlimited opportunities to get stunning creative items at unbelievably low prices as compared to eBay prices. The dropship business need not buy these items, but an arrangement could be worked out for working on commission. They will likely be happy to take his payment and deliver the products to the buyer of the dropship business when a sale is made.

WHAT IS DROPSHIPPING?

What is Dropship?

Dropship is a new outstanding and smart way to sell goods online.

1. Suppliers, makers, manufacturers, traders who want to extend their sellings online, widening their business horizon in a very simple and quick way, contacting directly thousands traders in the web.

2. Managers of e-commerce, sellers on eBay and online sellers who want to expand their own online list without any investment or to advance money which is usually needed for buying the products in order to cut totally all the start-up costs and warehouse one. You will have the chance to choose any product to sell to the Dropship suppliers that you will find on the OpenDropship site. You will be finally able to focus exclusively on the selling and the sponsorization of the product cutting also time and costs due to the shipment and delivery

How does Dropship work?

Dropship is a new system: a seller chooses a product to sell to the Dropship suppliers registered on the OpenDropship site. The seller can add the product to sell on his own site or on other sites like eBay, without buying it in advance. This method is useful because the seller can copy the images from the OpenDropship site and he can add them directly on the other sites and social network as well as the ecommerce sites in order to have more visibility. When the product is sold, the seller will directly notify the supplier. As last step, the supplier will directly send the product to your costumer. Your earning is decided upon the percentage on each product, previously decided with the supplier. The percentage is different and varies from one to another merchandise category.

What is OpenDropship?

OpenDropship is the first Dropship Marketplace; it's a virtual market which bounded customers sellers and suppliers interested in this new system. It's the right meeting point between the web customers and the web sellers on internet.

Dropshipping has become a very popular concept and lots of goods are sold to customers with the help of this concept. Dropshipping is a supply chain management technique where a retailer does not keep the goods he is selling in stock. When you buy a product from such a retailer he will transfer the order directly to the manufacturer or to a wholesaler and the goods are then delivered directly to you. A lot of people may not even be aware that they have bought goods that will be dropshipped. In this article we will find out more about how dropshipping works and what you should consider before selecting the right dropshipper.

Once a retailer receives an order from a customer he will forward this order to a wholesaler or to a manufacture and they will then ship the goods directly to the customer. As with any other retail business the retailer makes his profit from the difference between the wholesale and retail price. Retailers who sell goods with the help of a dropshipper will often keep show items in the store which the customer can inspect. These show items are usually exactly like or very similar to the product that will finally be delivered to the consumer. Some retailers may only provide a catalogue or a website from which the customer can select his product.

Sometimes retailers prefer to hide the fact that they will be dropshipping the goods to avoid stigma. This is achieved with the help of 'blind shipping' where goods are delivered without a return address. Sometimes retailers will use 'private label shipping' in which case the merchandise will have the return address of the retailer even though it shipped from somewhere else. Dropshipping is used a lot by small businesses and in online auctions. A lot of custom products are dropshipped to the customer. Sometimes even retailers who keep stock end up drop shipping an order if the order is very large.

The main advantage of dropshipping is that it eliminates a lot of handling and inventory costs. Since one wholesaler or the manufacturer himself will be packing and shipping the products a lot of handling and inventory costs are eliminated. This leads to the customer getting the product at a reduced price. As with any other business there are risks involved with dropshipping as well. One of these risks is backordering. Once the retailer forwards the order to the wholesaler it may happen that the goods are sold out. This will mean that the customer will have to wait a long time to receive the goods. This will reflect badly on the retailer. When you are starting a new business and selecting a dropshipper you should look at what kind of availability guarantee the dropshipper is providing. You need to keep in mind that you are selling goods without having them on hand. You need to be assured that the dropshipper will have the goods available once you have sold them to a customer.

BENEFITS OF DROPSHIPPING

Lower Capital Requirement

For many retailers, one of the toughest aspects of starting a business is figuring out how to approach inventory. Traditionally, merchants spend thousands of dollars on inventory investment, which can significantly eat into a business's starting capital. With dropshipping, however, you don't have to buy products or worry about low stock. Starting a dropshipping company means reduced upfront costs, less stress, and fewer responsibilities, with more time and money to allocate to other aspects of your growing business.

Flexible Location

Today's customers demand unparalleled shipping, quick to dissolve their relationship with businesses that fail to meet their expectations. By using a dropshipping company, your business can gain a geographic advantage. Businesses located in the Central U.S. can benefit from a supplier located on the West Coast, and vice versa. Having your products close to the customers who buy them puts you in a position to ensure your brand can deliver exceptional service from the point of order all the way to delivery.

Save time and money

Running a dropshipping empire means that your business won't be burdened with the hassles of managing and paying for a warehouse. You won't need to track inventory, handle returns, or restrict your office to a particular location. As long as you have an internet connection to stay in touch with your suppliers and customers, you have the freedom to take your business anywhere and everywhere across the globe.

Wider Product Selection

Because merchants are typically required to pre-purchase their products, it's usually easier and cheaper to purchase a select few items in larger quantities than to offer a diverse selection. But with dropshipping, you can sell however many products you want on your online store without having to worry about inventory or costs.

Reduced Risk

Starting a business comes with many risks, not the least of which is the thousands of dollars you'll potentially invest in inventory. With a dropshipping model, if things don't pan out the way you planned, you can make a relatively clean break, without fear of being stuck with thousands of dollars worth of inventory.

REASONS TO CONSIDER DROP SHIPPING

Drop shipping is an order fulfillment strategy where the retailer does not keep products in inventory, but relies on wholesalers or manufacturers to actually ship orders to customers. This arrangement has several advantages that make it attractive to online merchants.

When a customer places on order for a drop shipped product online, the retailer receives the order and payment for the order, and then either automatically or manually contacts the wholesaler or manufacturer, issuing a purchase order for the item and providing instructions for shipping directly to the customer. The wholesaler or manufacturer ships the product, and the retailer earns a profit.

There are at least five good reasons that almost any ecommerce retailer should consider drop shipping. Unfortunately there are some "gotchas" to consider too.

1. A Broad Product Offering

Drop shipping allows merchants to offer many more products for sale than what might be feasible if that merchant had to inventory everything.

Imagine a retailer who sells specialty coffee and tea both online and in a boutique. The physical store might have limited space for storing espresso machines, so that the retailer may only offer one or two models in store. But online, if the retailer has drop-shipping arrangements in place with several espresso machine makers, that retailer might offer dozens of different options.

Having a broad range of options can also help marketing, since each product page can be a landing page, entry in a comparison-shipping engine, or additional page for Google or Bing to index. These additional products are a way of introducing a greater number of potential customers to the store.

2. Come to Market More Quickly

While it takes just as long to post a drop-shipped product to an ecommerce platform as it does a product that is in inventory, drop shipping may help a merchant come to market more quickly.

Drop shipping eliminates wait times when products are shipped from the distributor or manufacturer to the merchant. In some cases, this can be a few weeks. With drop shipping, a merchant can start selling the moment the product is published on the ecommerce site.

3. Explore New Lines

Drop shipping gives merchants a way to test new products without having to bring in inventory.

For example, imagine a retailer that sells tack — saddles, bridles, and other equine-related products — for what is called "Western" style riding. Occasionally, this online retailer gets requests for "English" style saddles or riding apparel. A drop shipping agreement with a supplier of "English" gear would allow the retailer to explore how well those products would sell, without committing hard dollars to the test.

4. Reduce Your Investment

An underlying theme in points 1 to 3 has been that merchants employing a drop shipping strategy don't have to keep products in inventory. Quite simply, since drop-shipping agreements generally do not require any upfront investment, a retailer can significantly reduce its investment in products.

This also means that some ecommerce start-ups don't need as much money as one might think to get up and selling.

5. More Time

In a drop shipping arrangement, the retailer does not receive, stack, store, pull, pack, or ship products. All of these tasks are time consuming, which means drop shipping saves time.

In a startup ecommerce business where the storeowner may also be the box packer, this additional time will be available to actually sell products, which should benefit the company. In larger operations, the timesavings may result in a reduction — or stabilizing — of labor costs.

PROS AND CONS OF DROPSHIPPING

PROS OF DROPSHIPPING

As a business model, dropshipping has several different aspects that prove to be beneficial, such as:

It's easy to set up: It doesn't take an entire village to set up since it essentially involves just 3 steps – find the supplier, set up your website and start selling the goods! To someone who is new to the ecommerce industry, this business model is relatively easy to understand and implement.

The cost of setting up your online business using the dropship model is next to nothing: In traditional business models, the majority of the costs are related to setting up and running the retail operations, i.e. purchasing the inventory. Since dropshipping eliminates that step, and thus the cost of it, all you have to pay for is the associated costs of running your website (hosting, theme, apps, etc.).

You don't have to worry about exorbitant overhead costs: As previously mentioned, the business owner is not required to purchase inventory thus the costs of renting or buying warehouse/office space and the other smaller yet substantial costs pertaining to it (electricity/phone bills, stationery, etc.) aren't an issue. The fixed costs of managing the website are all that a business owner has to worry about.

The risk of drop shipping as a business model is significantly lower: If the business doesn't sell products it still doesn't lose anything, so there is little to no pressure about having to sell your inventory.

The business can be run from anywhere thus the business owner is location independent: No office, no warehouse, no employees and no hassles. Little to no commitment to a physical space means that you could be sitting at a beach, sipping on mojitos while still turning profits. All you need is your laptop and the internet.

There is lots of variety when it comes to the products you want to sell: There is a drop ship supplier for almost anything that you would like to sell! You can rely on one great product, sell several products at once or mix it up; it's all up to you. Find your niche and there is bound to be a supplier that caters to it.

More time and resources to scale your business: In traditional retail business models, if you want more profits you have to do more work and invest that much more of your resource pool. With dropshipping all you have to do is send more orders to your dropship supplier and then let them handle everything else while you earn the profit and are left with more time to develop your business plans and scale!

Reduced losses on damaged goods: Since the shipment goes directly from the supplier to the customer, there are fewer shipment steps involved which drastically reduce the risk of damaged items while moving from one physical space to another.

CONS OF DROPSHIPPING

Just like everything in life, there are some disadvantages that come along with the many advantages of dropshipping. Here are a few cons to the dropship business model:

Slightly lower profit margins in comparison to sourcing from a wholesaler or manufacturer: Depending on your niche, location or requirements, suppliers and vendors will charge you higher prices for dropshipping products, which do eat into your profit margins.

Complete liability when something goes wrong, even when it is the supplier's fault: Since the customer is purchasing the product from the retailer's website, if the supplier messes something up, it's still the retailer's fault as the brand is the face of the retail process. This is one of the reasons why it is incredibly important to choose the right supplier.

The brand has a significantly lower level of control: Customer satisfaction is often linked to the details – personalized packaging and branding of the shipped products, freebies and notes accompanying the order – it's almost always the smaller things that count. Unfortunately, the drop shipping model seldom affords retailers the opportunity to control how their brand is presented during the delivery and fulfillment process as the supplier is the one who ships the products. However, there are some suppliers who may be willing to go that extra mile – be advised, it may cost you though.

Certain issues may arise due to complexities with shipping: selling multiple products may seem like a good way to drive up sales and make a substantial profit, but this could actually be counter-intuitive if the retailer has multiple suppliers for these products. Different suppliers will charge different shipping costs depending on factors like location, type of products, etc. If a customer orders multiple products which ship from different suppliers, the retailer will have to work out and pay the shipping costs separately. Transferring these varying shipping costs on to the customer may negatively affect conversion rates, thus, in turn, impact the profit margins.

Level of competition is relatively high: The attractiveness and popularity of the dropshipping business model means more and more retailers in every segment and niche. Unless a retailer is catering to an extremely specific segment or niche, the competition could possibly be detrimental.

Managing the inventory can be tricky: keeping track of the stock of the supplier is nearly impossible. Miscommunications can cause issues such as cancellations and having to place orders on back order. This aspect can, of course, be managed with software these days but those too come at a price and may increase your overhead and fixed costs

DROPSHIPPING MYTHS

Drop shipping is not a new idea. Yet the concept of suppliers fulfilling direct to consumer rather than to a retailer has failed to gain momentum for some retailers due to unfounded fears around suppliers' not being willing and able to match customer expectations and the resource investment required to manage a drop-ship model. Yet with growth plateauing, warehouse costs spiraling and the younger, digital-first generation becoming ever harder to attract, drop shipping offers retailers the chance to achieve essential business objectives: expand both product range and customer base.

Despite the inherent flexibility, many UK retailers are still prejudiced against drop shipping due to a number of outdated myths.

Myth #1: Suppliers don't care

Retailers are passionate about retaining control over every aspect of the customer experience – for good reason. But the perception that drop shipping cannot emulate the retailer's own model, from order lead time to visibility of stock availability, is archaic. The idea that suppliers are not committed to delivering an exceptional level of customer service is simply not true. Indeed, with growing numbers of brands and suppliers now opting to go direct to consumer, many suppliers can now offer service levels that rival those of retailers.

Myth #2: Quality of experience is compromised

Quality of customer experience is at the heart of every logistics operation; from retailers to suppliers and third-party logistics providers, an inability to respond to changing customer demands is a fast track to business failure.

Of course, no retailer can afford a spike in calls to customer services as a result of missing orders, or the additional resources required to micromanage multiple supplier relationships. But the perception that drop ship cannot be controlled is based on past attempts that relied on legacy technology and failed to provide real-time visibility of the entire order and shipment process.

Legacy technology constraints are no longer an issue. Cloud-based drop-ship hubs provide a single source of information for both suppliers and retailers. Retailers can track supplier performance in real-time, providing excellent control and contract enforcement; while access to an intuitive, cloud-based drop shipping solution provides an efficient route to new markets. A win-win for both parties.

Myth #3: Drop shipping is resource intensive

Given current financial constraints, no retailer wants to invest in a team of full-time employees to manage drop shipping – and there is no need. With complete visibility into every supplier's inventory, as well as the order processing status, drop shipping can be managed by exception.

In addition to proactive supplier management, immediate, accurate information and exception-based drop-ship models support a far more proactive retail model. For example, a retailer can set an automated alert if an order hasn't been shipped within 24 hours, even if the contract demands 48-hour shipment. At this point, a retailer can opt to intervene or trust the supplier to meet the target.

Myth #4: Questionable business case

In a fast-evolving retail model, determining the business case for any significant investment is critical. With many retailers recognizing the need to overhaul existing fulfillment models, including new warehouse space and investment in automation, it is interesting to note the rapid ROI that can be achieved by adding drop shipping to the business model.

With the spiraling cost of UK warehouse space, any inventory reduction can offer an immediate return. This approach also offers a new level of business agility and innovation, enabling retailers to quickly test new products and categories without expensive investment in stock. The category mix can be reconsidered to include, for example, products that are not currently stocked due to size, cost or complexity.

The whole approach adds an essential level of agility to the business, while the ability to shut space and expand the customer assortment offers an immediate bottom line value.

Conclusion

Without an expanded and evolving product assortment, growth can be tough to achieve. Retailers need to consider another model; a way of expanding what they offer to customers without incurring additional inventory and warehousing costs. Adding drop shipping to the mix provides the chance to significantly extend the assortment mix and add categories to the portfolio, without significant capital outlays. The model is incredibly compelling, especially in the UK market with its spiraling warehouse costs.

Successful drop shipping can transform retail fortunes. It does require a mindset shift, but the perceived barriers of service quality and lack of information visibility have been eradicated. Suppliers are both willing and able to replicate, and even exceed, the level of customer service offered by retailers; and immediate access to stock and order information enables an exception-based management model that not only enforces standards but also minimizes resources and operational costs.

FACTS ABOUT DROPSHIPPING

1. The webstore facts:

The main source markets: Europe and USA

The rating of top-5 countries most actively placing orders in our stores is comprised of:

USA: California; Florida;

Canada: Alberta; Ontario;

Germany;

UK;

Australia.

Apart from that, a rising demand for our products from customers in Asia and Africa can also be seen quite clearly. When you know your main source markets, you have an opportunity to optimize your marketing efforts, and also consider payment and delivery issues carefully. It is vital for your supplier to arrange shipments to these regions, and it is crucial for your dropshipping store to support the payment methods that are most typically used in these countries.

Average revenue per webstore visitor: $0.43

To get this figure, we take the total revenue we got from all the processed sales, and divide it by the total number of Internet users who visited our stores. It lets us understand whether our stores' offers and design are appealing enough for our customers and whether they are motivated enough to make a purchase from us.

Day of the week with the largest amount of sales: Saturday

It is quite important for us and for every dropshipping store owner to know the days of the highest customers' activity since it defines the strategy of promoting the stores via shout-outs and other ways of social networks use.

Day of the week with the lowest amount of sales: Wednesday

Knowing which days normally are not characterized with a significant amount of placed orders, we can flexibly adjust the working schedule of our staff members, and use this free time to focus on managing customer relations, dealing with promotional tasks, thinking through marketing strategy, etc.

Core traffic sources that attract the largest number of visitors:

Social media;

Organic traffic;

Paid traffic (Google Adwords).

Apart from these, SEO also plays a significant role in generating the desired amount of traffic. Since our stores generally have a wide range of products, they are indexed by search engines and get good rankings on search engine result pages.

It is vitally important for drop shippers to know the main sources of traffic for their webstores. This kind of information gives them an opportunity to evaluate and increase the efficiency of all the steps taken to boost the traffic.

The most efficient traffic sources that attract the largest number of buyers:

Paid search – 2, 43% conversion rate;

Organic search – 2, 20% conversion rate;

Direct – 1, 40% conversion rate.

The previous parameter shows what sources bring us more visitors, and this one shows the efficiency of the measures we take to turn these visitors into actual customers. Again, this type of data helps us rethink and redefine the strategies we use if necessary.

The amount of time necessary to achieve 100k likes on Facebook: 9 months

While promoting one of our stores in social networks, we were able to achieve 100 000 likes on its dedicated Facebook fan-page. During the first 6 months of the page existence, it managed to get only 10 000 likes, but after reaching this milestone we decided to implement a new promotion strategy which is described in detail in this article, and in 3 months the number of likes increased from 10 000 to 100 000. It gives us the reason to consider this strategy successful, and to recommend it to our customers who order their own stores from us.

2. The payment and shipping facts

The most popular delivery option: ePacket

The concept of ePacket delivery was purposely created for small packages not weighing more than 2 kg (4.4 lbs) and costing less than $400. This system allows a really prompt and quite cheap delivery which is exceptionally convenient for buyers – they don't have wait for weeks for their order to arrive, and they don't have to bear extra costs. Additionally, the shipment movement can be monitored with the help of tracking codes provided by the supplier.

Knowing that ePacket is so popular with our customers and for the vast majority of Internet shoppers worldwide, we pay a special attention to choosing our suppliers – we need to be 100% sure they provide this shipping option.

The most popular payment methods:

Credit cards – 60%;

PayPal – 40%.

It is vital to know what kind of payment method your customers prefer, and what payment options are available within the country the order comes from. But it is even more important to integrate the necessary payment system in your dropshipping store – you surely want your buyers to have no technical or any other problems while paying for their purchases.

3. Customers' profile facts

Gender distribution of purchasers:

Female buyers – 58%;

Male buyers – 42 %.

Surely enough, this statistics is highly important since it gives us the opportunity to target our potential customers more efficiently. We give a thorough consideration to this parameter while planning our advertising campaigns on Facebook, in Google Adwords, etc.

The average number of items per one order: 2, 5 items

What's the most important about this parameter is its change within some period of time? This dynamics matters if you implement the techniques of upselling (you try to persuade a customer to buy a more expensive improved variation of a chosen product) or cross-sell (you try to persuade a customer to buy a complimentary item from another product category). The change in the average number of items per order helps you understand whether your strategy is working as planned.

4. Demand patterns facts

Best selling clothes size: XL

Best selling clothes colors: black and grey

Best selling clothes type: hoodies and sweatshirts

Most demanded clothes material: cotton

Best selling model of phone case: iPhone 5

Best selling jewelry type: necklaces

Best selling lifestyle items: keychains, mugs, and watches

Most demanded type of products: interactive goods (items with highlight, self-stirring mugs, etc.)

Products that have seasonal demand: scarves, hats, and gloves (bought in late autumn); backpacks (bought before the start of school season); fancy cosplay costumes (bought before Halloween).

This kind of statistic is extremely important not only for our product strategy when we decide what to include in our stores offer: it also impacts our promotional efforts. For example, knowing that grey and black clothes are bought substantially more often than colored ones, we try to set an appropriate main photo on the product page of an item that is available in several colors.

5. Support facts

Most typical questions our support team gets asked:

When will my order arrive?

Where is my order?

Where is my tracking?

Knowing what types of questions are asked most frequently, we can prepare the answers in advance in order to facilitate our customer relations management and make the communication process easy and comfortable for both sides.

WHO AND WHO SHOULDN'T VENTURE INTO DROPSHIPPING?

Who is Dropshipping For?

Dropshipping is a pretty great business model for a first timer who is just dipping their toes into the online business world. It's attractive to a novice as it's a low-risk and low-investment way of starting your own business, thus, doesn't feel like so much of a gamble.

Since the amount of capital that needs to be invested into this business model is minimum, it is also ideal for someone who is already a store owner with an inventory but is looking to try out particular products in the market to see how well it does before stocking up on it. If you're interested in learning more about this, check out our How to Test Product Ideas with Dropshipping When You Don't Dropship post.

For someone who is expecting amazing margins right off the bat, this business model may be disappointing. If profit is your primary interest then you'd be better off going straight to the source – i.e. the manufacturers – but manufacturers don't always facilitate dropshipping. Since dropshipping profit margins are also considerably lower in comparison to other business models such as manufacturing and wholesaling, dropshipping would perhaps not bode well with a brand that is a new startup, as the business doesn't have the ultimate control when it comes to customer satisfaction through branding and brand experience.

There are a few types of entrepreneurs that the drop shipping model will work well for. Let's take a look at some of them:

Validating Entrepreneur: Drop shipping can be a great way to test new products, or even a new startup, before investing heavily into inventory that may not sell, making this the perfect business model for the entrepreneur that requires a high level of business and product validation before investment.

Budget Entrepreneur: Drop shipping is definitely the least expensive method of selling online because you don't have to purchase any inventory upfront. Because of this, the drop shipping method works well for entrepreneurs who have a limited budget or would prefer to keep startup costs as low as possible.

First Time Entrepreneur: The drop shipping model for selling online also is a good business model for someone just starting out selling online. The fact is selling online isn't easy. Driving traffic and converting that traffic for the average marketer can take a long time to figure out and optimize. Because of the low costs associated with starting a drop shipping business, it allows new entrepreneurs to start to learn the ropes of setting up a store, driving traffic and conversion optimization before investing thousands (or more) in inventory that you may get stuck with.

Walmart Entrepreneur: Drop shipping is also for the person that wants to sell a wide variety of products and models. Depending on what the price range is of the products you intend to sell, or if you want to sell hundreds or thousands of different products, it's nearly impossible without massive funding to acquire that entire inventory. In this case, drop shipping would be the appropriate model because, again, you don't need to purchase inventory upfront.

Who Isn't Drop Shipping For?

There are also a few types of entrepreneurs that drop shipping isn't for:

Brand-Centric Entrepreneur: Building a long-term sustainable brand is difficult but the rewards can be incredibly worthwhile. However, building a brand while utilizing the drop shipping business model is exponentially more difficult as there are so many elements of the entire customer experience that you won't be able to control. For example, many times you may find out that after a customer has purchased something from you it's sold out with your drop shipper. This leaves you in the uncomfortable and frustrating position of trying to coordinate between your customer and your drop shipper and can become a really poor experience for your customer. Another point to keep in mind is because you're not shipping the product yourself you don't have any control over the experience of your customer receiving the package. Almost 100% of the time it's going to be the product in a big brown box with packing peanuts. You need to ask yourself if that's the experience you want your customers to have. Finally, because you don't ship the products yourself you don't own the relationship with the shipping companies. When something does go wrong and your customer doesn't receive the package you can't simply call UPS and get the situation corrected. You need to coordinate this with a busy account rep which could take days to sort out, again, leaving your customer with a bitter taste in their mouth.

Margin Focused Entrepreneur: Probably the biggest problem with the drop shipping business model is the razor-thin margins. Generally, for traditional drop shipping products and companies your gross margins (the price you sell it for minus the cost you pay your drop shipper) are around 10-20%. At the end of the day when you pay your credit card transaction fees, shipping cart, email service, and other app fees you will be looking at only a few percent. There is a fair share of online entrepreneurs running 1 million dollar revenue per year drop shipping businesses that at the end of the day are making 40-50k profit.

Non-Creative Marketers: Most manufacturers (which can also be drop shippers of their own products) have sales goals in which 30% of the sales need to come from direct-to-consumer sales, usually through their own ecommerce site. This means that if you're selling their products, you will be competing directly with your own supplier, a supplier that is able to have much higher margins than you on the very same products. Any chance of competing head-to-head against them is pointless. They will almost always win because they can afford to. If you're going to beat your own supplier you need to be creative and find and exploit channels they aren't using to acquire customers. If your only ideas are to use Google Adwords and Facebook Ads, you're likely out of luck.

HOW TO START A DROPSHIPPING BUSINESS

Identify a Market

In dropshipping, you and your competitors all have access to the same products and work with suppliers that offer similar levels of service. Therefore, the great differentiator between your business and your competition will be your marketing efforts. To market successfully, you need to identify a target demographic and sell a product that speaks to them in some way.

Here are some things to keep in mind as you refine your business concept:

What interests you: It's easier to sell what you know. Consider your own interests when looking for a product to sell. Chances are if you like it, other people are into it too.

Identify a niche: When you first start, you want to focus on a smaller subset of people because you can tailor your business to meet their specific needs. An example of a niche would be people who practice tae kwon do, or pescatarians. Ideally, you'll find a niche and a product that already interests you.

Keyword research: To help you identify a niche, you should perform keyword research via Google Adwords and Trends to see if there is any search volume around the products you wish to sell. The higher the search volume, the higher the demand for that product.

See what's selling online: Another way to find products in demand is by checking "best selling" lists on major ecommerce marketplaces like Amazon and eBay.

Social media engagement: Check to see what people in your niche are engaging with on major social media platforms, like Reddit, Facebook, and YouTube.

Competition research: Once you've found a niche, research the competition in that space. If high demand is already being met with high supply, you'll want to steer clear of that market.

Evaluate profitability: Finally, once you have identified a market and a product, you're going to want to evaluate the profitability of your concept. With dropshipping margins being so low, you want to ensure you can actually make money in your niche. The dropship supplier directory SaleHoo recommends selling a non-seasonal product that is not dominated by major brands, cheap to ship, and retails for at least $15.

Find a Supplier

Once you settle on a niche you want to target with a specific product, it is time to find a supplier that sells that product. This shouldn't be hard as there are many different dropship suppliers that offer millions of different products.

Your dropship supplier is a key partner in your business. To help you find the right one, we recommend prioritizing the following criteria:

Experience: You want to make sure your supplier has a proven track record in the dropshipping business and also provides good customer service. Before reaching out, look up their Net Promoter Score and see what's being said about them on review websites like TrustPilot and Better Business Bureau.

Fees: With margins being so low, you want a dropshipper that won't hit you with unreasonable fees. SalesHoo says you shouldn't pay more than $5 per item for stocking, packaging, and shipping. Some dropshippers will also charge you a small monthly fee for working with them.

Fast shipping: With dropshipping, the expectation is that the product will arrive within one to two weeks (most dropshippers are located in China). Any longer and you will likely face backlash from your customers.

Product samples: A major occupational hazard with dropshipping is suppliers that sell products of low quality. Before contracting with any supplier, you should request and receive samples of the products you wish to sell.

Referrals: A good supplier will provide you with referrals to other businesses they work with upon request. If they refuse, consider it a red flag.

Now that you know what to look for in a supplier, let's talk about the two types of suppliers you can work with: dropship marketplaces and manufacturers.

STEPS TO BUILDING A SUCCESSFUL ONLINE DROP SHIPPING BUSINESS

Drop shipping is an extremely popular business model for new entrepreneurs, especially gen Zers and millennials, due to internet marketing skills far outweighing financial capacity. Since you don't need to stock or handle the items you are selling, it's possible to start a drop shipping business with limited funds.

An ecommerce website that operates a drop shipping model purchases the items it sells from a third-party supplier or manufacturer, who then fulfills the order. This not only cuts operational costs, but it also frees up your time to focus all of your efforts on customer acquisition.

If you are ready to start a business that can compete with retail giants, and do so on a limited budget, then follow the six steps below. While it doesn't take a lot of startup funds to launch a drop shipping business, it will require an immense amount of hard work.

1. Select a niche.

The niche you select needs to be laser-focused and something you are genuinely interested in. A product range that isn't focused will be difficult to market. If you aren't passionate about the niche you select, you will be more apt to becoming discouraged, because it takes a lot of work to successfully scale a drop shipping business. Here are some points to consider when selecting your niche:

Seek attractive profits. When you are running a drop shipping business model, your focus is on marketing and customer acquisition, so the amount of work required to sell a $20 item is essentially the same as it would be to sell a $1,500 item. Select a niche with higher-priced products.

Low shipping costs are very important. Even though your supplier or manufacturer will handle the shipping, if the cost is too high, it will act as customer repellant. Find something that is inexpensive to ship, as this also gives you the option of offering free shipping to your customers and absorbing that cost as a business expense in order to attract more sales.

Make sure your product appeals to impulse buyers with disposable income. When you are focused on driving traffic to your website, you want to experience the highest conversion rate possible because most visitors will never return. The products you are selling should trigger impulse buys and appeal to those with the financial ability to make a purchase on the spot.

Make sure people are actively searching for your product. Use Google's Keyword Planner and Trends to check some common search terms related to your potential niche. If nobody is searching for what you are planning on selling, you are dead in the water before you even begin.

Create your own brand. Your drop shipping business will have more value if you can rebrand whatever it is you are selling and pass it off as your own. Look for a product or line you can white label and sell as your own brand with custom packaging and branding.

Sell something that isn't readily available locally. Pick something your customer can't find down the street. That way, you become more attractive to a potential customer.

2. Perform competition research.

Remember, you will be competing with other drop shipping operations as well as retail giants such as Walmart and Amazon. This is where a lot of potential drop shippers go wrong, because they look for a product that has little to no competition. That's a sign there isn't demand for that particular product.

There are many reasons why a product might not have a lot of competition, including high shipping costs, supplier and manufacturing issues or poor profit margins. Look for products that have competition, as it's a sign that there is a high demand and the business model is sustainable.

3. Secure a supplier.

Partnering with the wrong supplier can ruin your business, so it's important that you don't rush this step. Conduct proper due diligence. Most drop shipping suppliers are located overseas, making communication extremely important, both in terms of response speed and the ability to understand each other. If you are not 100 percent confident in the communication abilities of a potential supplier, move on and continue your search.

Alibaba has become one of the largest online resources to identify and communicate with potential manufacturers and suppliers. Make sure to ask a lot of questions and learn what their production capabilities are in the event that your business grows exponentially. You want to be certain they have the ability to scale with you.

Try to learn from other entrepreneurs who have walked this path in the past. There are plenty of information sources available, from business and tech blogs to this subreddit about drop shipping. It's a popular topic that can help you avoid costly supplier mistakes.

4. Build your ecommerce website.

The fastest way to launch a website that supports a drop shipping business model is to use a simple ecommerce platform such as Shopify. You don't need a tech background to get up and running, and it has plenty of apps to help increase sales.

Even if you have a sizable budget that would allow you to hire a web design and development company to create a custom solution, it's a much wiser move to use one of the plug-and-play options, especially in the beginning. Once you are established and the revenue is coming in, then you can explore additional website customization.

5. Create a customer acquisition plan.

Having a great product and a website is great, but without customers looking to buy, you don't have a business. There are several ways to attract potential customers, but the most effective option is to start a Facebook ad campaign.

This allows you to generate sales and revenue right from the start, which can contribute to quick scaling. Facebook allows you to place your offer directly in front of a highly targeted audience. This gives you the ability to compete with the largest brands and retailers immediately.

You also have to think long term, so search engine optimization and email marketing should also be a focus. Collect emails from the start and set up automated email sequences that offer discounts and special offers. It's an easy way to leverage your existing customer base and generate revenue without additional advertising and marketing spend.

6. Analyze and optimize.

You need to track all of the data and metrics available to grow your business. This includes Google Analytics traffic and Facebook conversion pixel data, if that is your main customer acquisition channel. When you are able to track every single conversion -- to know where the customer originated from and what path they took on your website that eventually led to a sale

-- it enables you to scale what works and eliminate what doesn't.

You will never have a set-and-forget advertising or marketing solution. You need to constantly test new opportunities and fine-tune current campaigns, which allow you to know when to optimize or shift campaign spend.

DROPSHIPPING SUPPLIERS

Drop shipping is the digital version of being able to "buy low and sell high" with minimal effort. You partner with suppliers that sell you an item at wholesale prices and you sell them to the buyer for the retail price.

With drop shipping, you only have to follow these simple steps to make money:

Partner with an online supplier

Post your product listings on various e-commerce platforms

The buyer makes a purchase and the supplier ships the item directly to the buyer

You never have to touch the physical product you're selling. When you make a sale, the product supplier will automatically ship the item from their warehouse to the customer.

Drop shipping is an exciting online side hustle because you sell items without handling the physical product. This income stream can be less time consuming than searching yard sales and thrift stores for items hidden treasures. Instead of spending time trying to build your inventory, you can spend building your drop shipping website and listing your products online to make your first sale sooner.

Although some drop shipping suppliers require an upfront financial commitment (think security deposit), drop shipping can still be cheaper than ordering in bulk and having to mail the items yourself. You will spend more time than money, building an online store and listing your products on the various online marketplaces to make a sale.

How to Find the Best Drop Shipping Suppliers

Becoming a successful drop shipper requires some initial effort. You will need to directly contact different manufacturers to discuss the partnership details.

When you drop ship, you should pursue these two different avenues for selling your items:

Create your own online storefront

Advertise your listing on e-commerce sites like Wish

The more places you list, the more audiences you reach. For example, think about your own group of friends and how many people exclusively shop on either Amazon or eBay. Drop shipping suppliers usually let you sell their products on multiple online marketplaces but some platforms make the listing and ordering process seamless.

1. Shopify

Shopify is probably the darling of drop shipping sellers because they are in "all-in-one" drop shipping platform. You can use Shopify for the following activities:

Partner with drop shipping suppliers

Create an online store

List your items on e-commerce marketplaces like Amazon and eBay

You can enroll in weekly drop shipping educational webinars and you can quickly add products to your store to begin selling immediately with Shopify's Oberlo app. Oberlo lets you list up to 500 products and make 50 sales for free each month.

Another advantage of using Shopify is that you can easily track each shipment in your storefront instead of relying on the supplier to email you the shipping details that you must manually enter into the shipping service website to track. Plus, you can sell your own physical or digital items if you have some to sell too.

So far, Shopify has helped drop shipping entrepreneurs like yourself complete more than 85 million sales!

2. BigCommerce

You can also use BigCommerce to create your own website and list your drop shipping items on other online marketplaces too. It's possible to directly connect with several drop shipping suppliers for free through BigCommerce. In other instances, you will need to do your own research to find suppliers and then list your products on your BigCommerce store.

Once you're ready to sell, BigCommerce can automatically list your products on the following online platforms:

Amazon

eBay

Facebook

Instagram

Pinterest

Google Shopping

You will enjoy 24/7 live agent support, shipping label discounts, and even the opportunity to have shoppers leave product reviews to entice future shoppers to make a purchase.

Tip: Dropship your own personally-designed clothing with CafePress. You upload the design and CafePress prints and ships the item directly to the buyer!

3. SaleHoo

One way to find drop shipping suppliers is to look for products on various online marketplaces and directly contact the manufacturer. The only problem is that this strategy takes time and you might be talking to a scam supplier.

With SaleHoo, you have instant access to a directly consisting of 8,000+ pre-vetted drop shipping suppliers. You can directly contact legitimate suppliers to forge a partnership.

A more valuable reason to use SaleHoo is their Market Research Labs. A key ingredient to making a steady income from drop shipping is picking in-demand products.

Shopping trends constantly change and using SaleHoo's research helps you stay a step in front of the competition. For example, you're probably not going to make as many sales by selling cassette tapes instead of a portable Bluetooth speaker. Although you can drop ship both of these items today, you still need to stay current with the times and preferable one step ahead.

Finally, SaleHoo also offers a community forum so you can gain advice and swap experiences with others. Newbies can also use SaleHoo's educational course to learn more about dropshipping too.

SaleHoo is an extensive directory but you still need to use an ecommerce platform like Shopify or

BigCommerce to effortlessly list your products online and notify the supplier when a sale is made.

4. Alibaba

Alibaba might be the largest online marketplace for finding drop shipping suppliers. Of course, buyers can also directly buy from Alibaba too.

Because drop shipping requires you to sell manufactured items, they are most likely going to be made overseas where production costs are significantly lower. That doesn't mean you can't find U.S.-based suppliers when you don't want to wait for a sold item to cross the ocean before it can be delivered to the buyer.

Alibaba lets you look for suppliers by region or top selected suppliers to quickly find a supplier that fits your criteria. To make sure you offer the quickest shipping times for overseas suppliers, only choose suppliers that offer "ePacket delivery" for delivery times of 30 days or less. Most international suppliers now offer this shipping option to remain a competitive buyer.

Don't forget that you can use the Shopify Google Chrome extension to quickly connect with suppliers too.

5. Doba

You can use Doba for their supplier directory and inventory management systems. It's possible to directly export product listings to your store and the other online marketplaces you sell on. Doba has four different plan options, but all levels have complimentary access to the following amenities:

Curated product category lists

Weekly deals email

Email support

Supplier report cards

If you want to export your product listing to Amazon and eBay, you will need to upgrade to an Advanced or Pro plan. Additional benefits of being an Advanced or Pro plan includes live chat support and the Elite Seller Report.

This monthly report shows you the top 30 products in each category. You can also access previous monthly reports to spot trends and see which products are a long-term success.

6. Worldwide Brands

Unlike some of the other drop shipping directories that charge a monthly or annual fee, Worldwide Brands only requires a single payment for lifetime access. You can access their directory consisting of more than 16 million products from over 8,000 suppliers.

Worldwide Brands also has an A+ rating from the Better Business Bureau! When you're dealing with supplier companies on the opposite side of the world that you may never visit in person, building a partnership through a reputable company speaks volumes.

You can filter vendors by the following traits:

Drop Shippers

Light Bulk Wholesalers

Large Volume Wholesalers

Instant Import Buys

Liquidation Deals

If you have more upfront capital, you might decide to try your hand at wholesaling too. Just keep in mind that you may have to rent warehouse space with the supplier so only pick products with larger profit margin or high popularity rating.

7. Wholesale2B

Wholesale2B offers more than one million drop ship products you can sell online. You can integrate your Wholesale2B partnerships with your store (i.e., Shopify or BigCommerce) and also directly list your items on other e-commerce platforms too.

You have many different direct export options with Wholesale2B, but you must purchase an individual subscription with each platform you want to use. For example, you need to pay $29.99 monthly for Amazon and another $29.99 for Shopify.

Although these automated plans are convenient, it can get expensive if you're not a high volume seller yet. You can also use their DIY Plan which only costs $67 a year.

Tip: You can also use Wholesale2B to directly drop ship on Bonanza too.

8. Sunrise Wholesale

Sunrise Wholesale also offers a Rolodex of drop shipping suppliers to create your own store and also sell on Amazon or eBay. The listings can also integrate with your Shopify and BigCommerce stores too.

They are also more affordable than some of the other recommendations mentioned on this list. Your best option is choosing an annual subscription for $99 to get full access to the Sunrise Wholesale platform.

With the Amazon and eBay tools, you can quickly analyze prices to make sure you competitively price your products. Your pricing power is very important as you can either lose money if you sell each item for a loss just to move your inventory.

You will also receive low inventory alerts and have access to phone, email, and live chat support too.

9. Inventory Source

Inventory Source integrates with more than 28 different online marketplaces. You can partner with more than 150 different suppliers for multiple product categories.

You also have access to several automation tools that let you quickly set the price, determine shipping prices, and you can also filter by product type when you need to view your store inventory.

When a sale is made, Inventory Source immediately notifies the supplier so you don't need to send an email or verify the purchase. And, they also handle the shipping information for you too. So, if you go on vacation, your drop shipping business can keep humming when you don't have reliable internet access.

10. Megagoods

Megagoods specializes in selling consumer electronics and video game items. Thankfully, these two categories are very broad so you shouldn't have an issue finding items that the average online shopper is looking for. For example, you can drop ship the obvious like flat screen TVs and phone chargers to other common household items like dinnerware.

Many items also offer free shipping, so you don't have to factor this cost into your final sales value. Although Megagoods, is a great site for drop shipping beginners, you might want to stop by to partner with common brands that offer good product quality.

11. National Dropshippers

National Dropshippers offers products that are 33% to 66% below the MSRP! If you can sell your products for the suggested retail price, you can make a minimum 33% profit on each item sold! You can use the product images and links from your partnerships on your own site or online marketplaces.

You can browse the available products by clicking the different product categories.

Some of the categories include:

Apparel

Cookware

Suitcases

Motorcycle

Outdoors

Perfumes

Pet Supplies

Not everything you drop ship has to cost $10 or less. These items can help you earn more money per sale because of their higher retail value.

12. Attend a Trade Show

Another way to connect with the best drop shipping suppliers is to attend a trade show. You can find local trade shows in drop shipping forums or an online Google search.

Trade shows are an excellent way to meet established and up-and-coming companies. You can also network by making personal contacts, feel and test the products you wish to sell, and even ask pertinent questions that can solidify a relationship.

Trade shows can also be more exclusive than combing a directly that any drop shipper (i.e., your competitors) can purchase access to. Although trade shows require more time and energy than contacting customers online, the extra effort can be well worth it.

13. See What the Competition is Selling

Some drop shipping supplier directories publish a bestseller list. This is one way to see which items other competitors believe are the best items to sell, but you can also search other online marketplaces to get ideas too. You should visit other drop shipping storefronts for the following reasons:

Find the most common suppliers

Compare prices

See if you can sell a product they aren't selling yet

Drop shipping is a competitive business and you need to know how your store stacks up against the competition. Making yourself different helps you gain a competitive edge over the other online drop shippers. You might all be selling the same product and the difference of a few cents in the sales price or a faster shipping option can mean all the difference in the world.

Avoiding Fake Drop Shipping Suppliers

Most online vendors are honest, but there's always a bad apple in every group. You need to follow these tips to make sure you don't partner with a fake drop shipping supplier that takes your money and runs.

Never Pay a Monthly or Annual Fee

Most legitimate suppliers require a small initial financial commitment. It might be $500 or $1,000, but this initial deposit serves as a credit for your initial sales. For example, if you need to commit $500, you don't have to give them additional money for the first $500 of inventory sold.

Fake suppliers may charge you a monthly fee. This isn't the industry norm and you should avoid these partnerships to protect your own seller reputation.

It's important to note that these fees are different than seller directory fees that websites like SaleHoo charge. Directories only connect you with suppliers and do not ship, warehouse, or manufacture the items you will be selling online.

Only Choose Supplier With Exceptional Feedback

Most directories and drop shipping platforms have a feedback rating for each supplier. To spare yourself a headache, only choose suppliers with a feedback score of at least 90%. Some drop shippers will even recommend a minimum rating of 95% depending on the platform.

You should also take the time to read the comments and to research the supplier information on a search engine before you strike a partnership. By using one of the recommendations above, the odds of finding a fake supplier are greatly reduced, but you should always maintain a wary eye.

Only Use "ePacket" or Well-Known Shipping Services

International shipping has greatly improved in recent years. Several countries now participate in a shipping program called "ePacket" that can take between five and thirty business days to deliver a product from a foreign warehouse to a U.S. buyer. Besides a quicker shipping time, you need to be able to track the package. Not knowing where the package is located means you will need to issue a refund and it may even disqualify you from seller protection benefits too.

Test Purchase a Product First

If you still think a supplier's reputation is questionable. You can start a partnership and make a test purchase. If the product arrives on-time and meets your expectations, they are most likely a legitimate supplier. If you're a first-time drop shipper, this test purchase also lets you walk through the ordering process from a buyer's perspective so you can make any modifications to your selling program too.

The Most Popular Products to Drop Ship

There are a few ways to determine the most popular drop shipping items. The easiest way is to view the most popular item lists that are published by your drop shipping store platform or directory.

You can also have success by conducting your own research. Besides visiting other drop shipper stores to see what they're selling, you can also visit Google Trends to get ideas.

Or, you can always try these "evergreen" product ideas too:

Beauty

Books

Clothing

Jewelry

Shoes

Watches

Phone cases

Phone repair kits

Portable chargers

Teeth Whitening

Toys

You're most profitable items will be the ones that are lightweight and affordable to ship. After all, shipping costs can be as much as the supplier price. But you always have to remember that you can't look at price alone. Consumer demand can be just as important, especially if a supplier requires a small deposit so you have some "skin in the game" to sell your inventory.

Drop shipping is a relatively new retail concept, but it can be very profitable if you don't want to deal with warehousing your inventory or manually shipping each item. You also don't need to spend a large sum of money to open your online store or partner with drop shipping suppliers. Although drop shipping requires work, it can produce a steady income as you secure multiple products and sell on several online marketplaces.

HOW TO SETUP A DROPSHIPPING STORE/WEBSITE

Ecommerce is estimated to be worth more than $20 trillion globally evidencing just how influential the internet has become when it comes to driving business forward. Every year several entrepreneurs are setting up their online store so as to be able to compete and reach their target audience. People spend most of their time today online and therefore having an ecommerce store could be the difference between you and your competitor.

Dropshipping is one of the most popular forms of practicing ecommerce today and the reasons are obvious. Dropshipping involves the retailer which is you selling products to your customers but your supplier or manufacturer handles the inventory, shipment and delivery of orders.

Why Create a Dropshipping Website?

Dropshipping can be very successful especially if you utilize a great strategy and select a good niche for your ecommerce business. Dropshipping only works if you have a great website which will serve as the link between you and your customers. The following are some of the reasons why you need a dropshipping website:

- Suppliers and manufacturers want to work with a reseller who can show they have an existing website and already have an existing customer base (however small). The website acts in your favor when looking for suppliers because they feel they can trust you will sell their products.

- All your competitors especially in dropshipping all have websites so why not you? Competitor analysis is a key component of ecommerce and therefore lacking a website could prove to be detrimental for your business.

- Most of your customers are online and having a website gives your business legitimacy.

- A website helps to showcase all the products and services that you offer in your niche.

How to Set Up a Dropshipping Website in 4 Steps?

The popularity of dropshipping can be attributed to the low startup costs and the reduced risk that the whole business model poses.

The model consists of three main elements namely the website which serves as the home for your products, the suppliers who ensure you don't suffer stock deficiencies and handle all your shipping requirements and lastly the customers who place orders and keep your business alive.

Most newbies often fear setting up websites because they have no experience in programming and assume that the cost of hiring a developer might be too expensive especially if they have a very small budget. Web development and ecommerce has significantly changed over the last decade and setting up a website is now easier than ever. Even without any experience in programming, there are several platforms today that teach people how to build dropshipping websites easily and some even do it for you in less than a day.

Assuming that you have already selected a niche and carried out intensive competitor analysis, the following steps should be followed when building your dropship website plan.

1. Identify an ecommerce website builder/platform

Building websites and ecommerce websites in particular has become extremely easy. Several companies offer website building services by either doing it for you or giving you templates/blueprints for you to edit and how to make a dropshipping website yourself. As with all softwares, different companies have better features than others and some are suited to different types of websites than others.

Depending on your budget, the type of platform you choose could easily determine how good your website is and how many functionalities you will have access to. Some of the most popular ecommerce platforms today include Shopify, BigCommerce, and WooCommerce by WordPress, Wix, Magento, Weebly, SquareSpace, 3dcart and Volusion. Each of these platforms has their own strengths and have different pricing models again based on the features and the target audience.

2. Get a domain name and hosting

The domain name is the name of your website on the www. This will be the name that will appear on the address bar of people's browsers when they search for your business online. A good domain name is short, simple and relevant to the type of business that you are doing. Domain names aren't very expensive and you should include the cost in your budget. The second thing is hosting, hosting basically means placing your website on the www.

It is what guarantees that your website actually exists on the internet. It also costs a certain amount based on the hosting provider that you choose and will have to be renewed after a certain period of time mostly a year. Some of the most popular hosting providers include BlueHost and GoDaddy. Always choose a hosting provider with fast servers and good reviews from existing customers.

3. Building the website

Shopify for example will want you to open an account and choose a price plan. They will then build a store for you but customization will have to be done for you. WooCommerce will require that you install

WordPress first before installing the WooCommerce plugin that is for ecommerce stores built using WordPress. For most platforms including Magento, Weebly, Wix and BigCommerce, they will only give you the layout of the site or give you a template to edit. Customization of the store is left up to you and will involve the following:

- Selecting a theme – most platforms have several themes that you can choose from and edit. Most of them are free but others will cost you some money depending on the features.

- Placing your logo on the site.

- Content – Ultimately what you place on the site will be left to you in terms of text and images or any other relevant content.

- General settings – Shopify for example wants users to setup their return and refund policies before they begin selling. Other settings include payment settings, shipping information.

- Structure – This is the dropship website design and while the platforms will provide the layout, you will have to consider the entire customer journey from the time of entering your site to placing an order and checkout. Most themes should give you builders that should make this easy. You should also research your competitors to see how they do it. Structure will make it easy for you to know which part of your website to place different types of content such as you're about page or FAQs section.

- Pages and categories – Most platforms will do this for you and you can add more pages if you need them. Most ecommerce sites have categories and sub categories for different product variations. Every category should have their own page.

- Additional widgets – These includes search, rss feeds, social media links, tags and several others.

- Plugins – Plugins are necessary if you want to have a robust website with advanced features and most of the good ones have a price but most of the essential ones are free.

- Security – This is a very important often overlooked. Most price plans for all platforms come with SSL certificates installed in your website.

- Blog – you may want to add a blog just so as to make your website more interesting. Most platforms can do this for you as well.

4. Finding a reliable dropshipper with suppliers

Your website is useless if you haven't identified a reliable dropshipper with suppliers that you will use to populate your store with products. There are many examples to look at such as Chinabrands, Aliexpress, Doba and others.

5. Add products to your website

The products are the main attractions of your website and therefore once you find reliable dropshippers you can add their product items to your site. Most of the best marketplaces have automated solutions or plugins that will allow you to import products to your website directly.

6. Edit product descriptions and images

For SEO purposes it may be wise to edit the product descriptions using your own words. Also if you have images you can use to depict the product well and good but using the supplier's images won't affect you as much because most product images often look the same.

7. Order system

Work on your order system and this means discussing with your supplier how they will handle shipments and whether the customer's billing address will be sent to them automatically. Discuss the entire supply chain.

8. Marketing

The website may be beautiful and dynamic but people will still need to find it. Marketing begins with competitor analysis and is a never ending process for ecommerce entrepreneurs. There are plugins that can help you for on-site marketing techniques but all the off-site techniques will be left to you. They include social media, blogging, email, events, flyers, word of mouth, referrals and many others.

Where to Get Dropshipping Website Templates/Designs?

• Theme Forest – All the dropshipping website templates on theme forest come at a cost with the cheapest going for $9. They have more than 50 templates available for dropshipping. The templates are compatible with most platforms including WooCommerce, BigCommerce and others.

• Shopify theme store – This is obviously for Shopify users and contains hundreds of themes. The theme store is very dynamic and features themes based on the niche of your business allowing your theme to tell the story of your business for you even before you place any content. Shopify has many free themes that are great for small businesses but has some that will cost you even more than $180. Such themes are mostly used by those entrepreneurs with large inventories.

- WordPress/WooCommerce – When you install WooCommerce on your WordPress, you will then gain access to several ecommerce themes and just like Shopify there are those that are free and others have a price.

- Wix/Weebly/Magento – All of these platforms will offer you themes both free and paid. Weebly has some free themes but they are very basic.

- Colorlib – Colorlib has templates that are designed using the bootstrap platform. All the templates are free and are based on different niches in ecommerce.

- TemplateMonster – As the name suggests, template monster has templates that are compatible with almost all CMS's including Joomla and MotoCMS. Since they feature templates for all the main ecommerce platforms, all the templates come at cost with most of them being over $100.

Must Have Dropshipping Plugins

1. Alidropship – A fantastic Aliexpress dropshipping plugin for WordPress users. It was established by the Alidropship Company for users who were importing products from the Aliexpress marketplace. Most of its features are automated. The plugin costs $89.

2. Oberlo – Oberlo is like a marketplace within a plugin and works best with Shopify. The app is on the Shopify app store and users can search the Oberlo marketplace to find products to import to your Shopify store. Oberlo is free.

3. Social Rabbit – This is another WooCommerce plugin that promotes your website on social media automatically after some configurations.

4. Mailchimp for Shopify – Mailchimp developed this app for Shopify users so that they could integrate their email marketing campaigns into the websites.

5. Alidropship woo – This is the WooCommerce version of the Alidropship plugin. It is more advanced and has enhanced features than the generic Alidropship. It also goes for $89.

6. Dropshix – Dropshix works well with Aliexpress and essentially gives feedback on shipping information. It's free.

7. Plugin SEO – Found in the Shopify app store. The free version of Plugin SEO gives you basic SEO improvement techniques by telling you if there are any issues with the performance of your website on search engines.

8. Content Egg – Another WordPress plugin, it became popular because of its robust features. Content Egg updates your product information and even allows auto-blogging.

9. Product Reviews – Shopify users can add this app on their website to allow customers to add reviews.

10. Chinabrands – The Chinabrands plugin can be considered the best because it is a one-time integration with your website and gives you all automated features for FREE.

Examples of Dropshipping Websites

Here are some dropshipping website examples that you can learn from to build a better dropshipping website.

• SoAestheticShop.com – one of the best-selling Shopify online stores in the world. This dropshipping website covers nearly everything from beauty, apparel items and accessories. The website serves several countries and accepts payments in more than 20 different currencies. It was founded by Justin Wong and now makes thousands of sales per month. Additionally, the company has an affiliate program and a partnerships program that help market the company worldwide.

• FashionNova – Just as the name suggest the website focuses on apparel items but with a particular focus on the trendiest and most fashionable clothing items. Located in the United States, the company website has great images with high resolution and is easy to navigate.

• MVMTWatches – they have free shipping worldwide hence the immense popularity of the store. They sell both men's and women's watches. They use a great theme that leaves visitors interested to look around the website.

• Wayfair – Deals with everything to do with home and living dealing in furniture, décor, bathroom and everything else. The store has been extremely successful even selling over 4 million in sales in one day at some point. Located in Boston in the USA, Wayfair works with several suppliers to ensure they never suffer stock deficiencies.

The Best Dropshipping Partners/Companies to Work With.

1. Chinabrands.com

As one of the largest distributors and online marketplaces in the world, Chinabrands has become a global powerhouse in dropshipping. The company is special due to its unique set of features that customers easily fall in love with. All resellers should want to work with Chinabrands for the following reasons:

• Excellent quality control – Suppliers are seriously vetted and so are their products to ensure only the highest quality make it to the marketplace.

• Automatic bulk listing – Chinabrands allows you to list all the products you need at once just with the click of a button on your website. Bulk listing allows you to populate your website faster.

• Pricing – Quality products at cheap and affordable prices.

• Wide range of products – With most manufacturers being based in China, you gain access to several variations of a product giving your customers a variety to choose from.

• Automated integrates with several sales channels regardless of the ecommerce platform you choose to work with including Shopify and WordPress.

• Automated inventory update in real time.

• Pricing automation and bulk price setting.

- Automated orders monitoring and Order auto-fulfillment.

- Global warehousing allows shipping to over 200 plus countries.

2. Aliexpress

Aliexpress is a sister company to ecommerce giant Alibaba but has made its name as one of the largest and most popular dropshipping platforms in the world. The platforms gives you access to hundreds of suppliers and millions of products for you to choose from. The products are very affordable at a low prices. Different suppliers offer different shipping rates and some are faster than others. Suppliers with the epacket filter are the fastest and most recommended.

3. Doba

Doba acts a liaison between retailers and suppliers by placing suppliers and manufacturers in one marketplace. The service is quite expensive for new entrepreneurs with the basic plan costing about $29 per month. Doba allows you to create your own custom lists.

Conclusion

New ecommerce entrepreneurs should not shy away from dropshipping as it can be very lucrative because of the reduced risk. Additionally, having a reliable dropshipper like Chinabrands by your side together with a dynamic dropshipping website could be the difference between success and failure. Build your own dropship website today!

STRATEGIES TO PROMOTE YOUR DROPSHIPPING STORE

When it comes to Dropshipping store, marketing is one of the most important elements of it. It is all dependent upon marketing that how many sales you will get.

There are so many advertising and promotion techniques that you could use to get success in your Dropshipping business. We will talk about some of these techniques and ways in this article today. Some of these techniques are personally tested by us.

1 – Facebook Advertising & Dropshipping

Facebook Ads are superb to us; likewise it is just a blessing from heaven to every advertiser trying to drive more guests. The things we have seen happening for me and for a few other drop shippers utilizing Facebook Ads is truly beguiling and this is something that we ask everyone (at any rate) experiment with.

You will require a financial plan for it, so if you have $0 then this may not be for you, but rather when you discover the outcomes we are getting with Facebook, at that point you will in the blink of an eye see why we trust that they are such a huge arrangement and we place them in those four systems to advertise your outsourcing shop. This is the thing that we ordinarily cover to promote in my shop Facebook:

How to Learn Facebook Advertising?

Like we said; you will need a financial plan. As should be obvious beforehand; we contributed a sum of $1000 last month however that isn't all. Get composed; get some exhortation, become familiar with the complexities of this stage and start testing. You don't have to end up a master with it. We question anyone is given the monstrous profundity and power it's, yet you need to know the essentials.

2 – Promoting Your Shop on Social Networking

Right, proceeding onward to societal sites, which; is an astounding route for you to advertise your outsourcing shop.

Starting at now, our social sites for my fall shipping shop involves three phases; Twitter Facebook and Pinterest and joined together, those 3 gets me around 40 percent of my general traffic.

Precisely like SEO, this can be 100% traffic. We should simply keep up the updates streaming on those stations and we are OK to utilize a helpful apparatus named Buffer for this. Buffer licenses you to plan person to person communication postings in advance so I'm never shy of getting substance and items being shared. In the season of composing this, we have got upgrades up to go for an additional 3 months.

It is route better to focus on a solitary web-based life and complete it very much contrasted more than 4 programs. Pick one, when we need to prescribe one, we would state Pinterest and focus on developing on the same platform.

Master TIP: Remember, when you begin getting guests in from person to person communication and SEO, you should start creating resemble the other alike-gatherings of people to your Facebook Ads that will drive down the expenses and (if) additionally support your transformations.

3 – SEO and Blogging

In the event that you are searching to acquire a quick buck with internet business, this isn't for you. Be that as it may, should you wish to develop an all the more long, feasible plan of action, at that point you have to start thinking about how to advance your Dropshipping search for SEO. Dropshippers (and eCommerce shops for the most part) fight a lot with SEO since the machine is developed against them.

For example; Amazon overwhelms the search results for practically any stock you may type into Google so extraordinary fortunes with attempting to fight with such an enormous brand with innumerable dollars in notices reserves of funds and a multitude of representatives.

Some of you might be wondering that what could be the solution in such case.

We have one possible solution with us. Become familiar with some Search Engine Optimization nuts and bolts and Begin using Shopify as a blogging device, It Is Going to require you some investment to discover what works best since it is distinctive for each market, however we will talk about the arrangement that I utilized myself: For Instance, If your outsourcing shop sells "yoga mats", your articles on the site ought to show up something like this:

"x points of interest of yoga"

"that the absolute best yoga mats for fledglings"

It is a long shot, yet in time and with persistence, at that point you are going to start getting gotten for a few catchphrases like this and it'll discover the ball moving for you.

How to build SEO for Dropshipping store?

When you begin getting guests to these articles, start to divert those endorsers of explicit item pages without anyone else shop. By method for example, the article "the absolute best yoga mats for apprentices" can include 20 distinctive yoga mats which you can connection to in your shop.

This is an incredible advance forward, and it'll get you traffic and profit and recollect; it is conceivable to make articles along these lines again and again. Clearly there is significantly more for this; however for the present future, doing the above can enable you to start.

To wrap things up, I Need to specify another Fantastic Way to advance your shop, this is the exceptionally discussed and discussed strategy of;

4 – Email Advertising

Indeed, email works great well, and it will add to heaps of offers that happen online rather than only for me by and by; in any case, for anybody realizes how to use it well.

Like social sites, You plan messages heretofore, in this manner, at this phase in time; you ought to have one month estimation of overhauls which are booked to wander out. Additionally, a mechanized grouping for every single supporter that joins a sound blend of accommodating articles and straightforwardly hard-move messages.

The absolute best thing that is worked so much is putting forth a 20% decrease to whoever joins my posting by methods for spring up when they arrive in my shop.

To conclude we would like to thank you all for perusing this article and we trust we've given you two or three proposals about how to best market your Dropshipping shop on the web.

DROPSHIPPING MISTAKES THAT CAN DESTROY YOUR BUSINESS

Dropshipping Mistake 1: Pricing Free + Shipping Items Too High

A 'free plus shipping' promotion gets super high conversions for the obvious reason that the item is free.

Well, kind of. The item isn't actually "free," as customers are required to handle shipping costs. But it's a bonus for the customers to get the item at zero cost, and it's definitely not the kind of sale you see every day.

This gives you, the dropshipper, and freedom in how you choose to price shipping. But more often than not, newbie dropshippers take advantage of this power and price their shipping way too high.

This is a very, very costly mistake.

When you sell an item and put a price on it, it is often ambiguous what the true value of the item is, because the customer has not manufactured the item themselves. They can't see how much you paid for it.

They don't know the true cost of the time, materials, or expertise that went into creating the product. That means you have a lot of flexibility in the price you can put on an item.

But when using the free-plus-shipping model, you can only price your shipping so high until customers start to detect something fishy is going on.

And customer's aren't stupid — they have most likely purchased an item online before, so they have a general awareness of how much shipping should cost.

That means you can't go and advertise an item as free plus shipping then put the cost of shipping at $20.

Of course, customers will give you some leeway for handling fees; but if you require them to pay $20 for shipping, your offer won't even been considered a good deal anymore, and they will end up bouncing.

Plus, think about it: wasn't your deal the reason the customer landed on your page in the first place? To price your shipping cost at an unreasonable price will only have customers bounce from your page, and leave you with no sale.

So how should you price the shipping? A good, safe price point for a free-plus-shipping promotion would be $9.95. This is a great price for shipping as:

Shipping fees usually cost around $10

It encourages customers to buy on impulse

Being greedy with shipping costs and pricing it higher than necessary only drives customers away, damages your store's reputation, and removes the possibility of making a sale.

Dropshipping Mistake 2: Not Building a Brand

Most new dropshippers focus simply on the initial sale.

This is the illusion most newbie dropshippers are fooled by — when in fact; the initial sale is NOT how most successful stores make their money: it is through upsells, cross sales, and promotions.

But none of this is possible without focusing on building a brand. This is the #1 priority every dropshipper must have if you want to build long-term success.

Your brand is what turns a one-off customer into a repeat customer; one that finds it hard not to return back to your store, because of the amazing value that you provide.

Building a brand earns your customer's trust; the biggest deciding factor of whether or not they end up clicking "Buy."

Ignoring your brand only hurts your ability to market new products to your customers since they won't have any trust built in you: they only bought your item based on their initial emotion, not because they LOVE your brand.

In other words, you have 'one-off' business. Your store relies on new customers to survive, as you do not care enough to nurture your existing ones.

As you can tell, these kinds of stores are very short-lived; they end up fizzling out sooner or later with nothing to show for it.

This obviously begs the question: How can you build a brand? A good brand is consistent in its:

Colors

Images

Message

When you think of unicorns, what colors come to mind?

Was it pink, purple, or a color similar to these? It was for me. Now imagine you ran a dropshipping store that sold only unicorn-related items — but the theme color for your site was black?!

That'd be pretty weird, as your theme color is clearly inconsistent with your niche. You always want to make sure to use colors that customers can associate with your niche.

The same goes for images. Using our unicorn example again, displaying images of bats certainly won't help express your brand, and it will confuse a lot (if not every) customer that comes to your store. Images of unicorns would be the ideal as that is what your site is dedicated to.

And, of course, the message must be congruent with your brand. You must make it clear in your copy what your store is about; whether that's on the homepage, the about page, or on the product pages.

One tip is to use keywords that your niche is familiar with. What jargon do people regularly use in your niche? For example, if you're into dropshipping, jargon like 'upsell' and 'funnel' are terms that make a lot of sense to you.

This also a sales weapon in disguise. By using familiar and buzz words in your copy, your customers are able to connect with you on a deeper level, and this goes a long way in building trust.

Dropshipping Mistake 3: Selling to Customers Outside of the USA as a Newbie

Newbie dropshippers tend to believe that by selling outside of the US, they will reach more customers and make more money!

On the surface, it makes perfect sense, right? Instead of limiting yourself to the U.S, you can reach out to millions of potential customers.

But this comes at a cost that newbie dropshippers aren't usually willing to make: a LOT more work.

You see, selling to other countries can be very lucrative — but as a newbie, it's a lot easier to start in the US, and then expand to other markets once you have more experience.

Why? Well, first, the U.S. market is HUGE! There are over 323 million people that live in the USA.

What that means is that there are tonnes of niche subgroups within the country that are interested in lots of niche things. So when it comes to the point where you are running ads to your store, it makes creating a targeted audience much easier.

The second reason is that shipping to the US is very reliable and trustworthy. The ePacket shipping option is handled by the United States Postal Service, unlike the ePacket shipping option to other countries which is mostly handled by China Post.

As a beginner in dropshipping, the best path to take is the one with least resistance — and this is a good thing! With more experience, you'll gain more confidence and be in a better place mentally to consider expanding out to other countries.

Dropshipping Mistake 4: Forgetting About Your Previous Customers

Most newbies assume getting new customers is what they should be focusing on to make money in their store.

And while it might seem this way, the real money is made in your email list.

To understand this, simply ask yourself: Would it be easier to make a sale from a new customer, or a customer who has already purchased from your store?

The answer is the latter. Why? You've already earned their trust! After all, they purchased from you before — what's to say they won't purchase from you again?

Most people completely neglect the power of remarketing even though it's a skill all the top dropshippers leverage.

And what's even crazier is ... these customers are free! Remarketing does not cost you anything, as opposed to acquiring a new customer which requires a lot of advertising.

In truth, repeat customers are worth WAY more in the long-term. Remember, they are in your email list where you can promote other items to them from your store.

So they won't end up just buying once, but several more times, which greatly increase the customer's true value. (Imagine a customer buying $200 worth of items throughout the year!)

Don't make the mistake of prioritizing trying to get new customers. Focus on leveraging the customers you already have by promoting other products they might have interest in purchasing.

Dropshipping Mistake 5: Being Afraid of Taxes

A lot of people ask the same question: "What about taxes? I can't start dropshipping because I don't know how to handle taxes."

Well, believe it or not, when you're dropshipping with suppliers, your sales tax obligations are very simple.

That is because your suppliers are based offshore in China. That means that you only have to collect sales tax in states where you have a big physical presence, which for many dropshippers will only be the state they live in (and if you don't live in the USA, the chances are you won't have to collect and pay any sales tax on USA-based sales!).

In addition, whether you're selling with Woocommerce or Shopify, collecting sales tax is easy, as both platforms have settings which will collect sales tax automatically for you.

So don't be afraid of this part — it's really simple.

If you want to learn more about your obligations for sales tax, we wrote a whole blog post dedicated to this topic.

Dropshipping Mistake 6: Not Having a Plan on How to Upsell Customers

If you're a regular reader of our blog, you know I can't stress enough the importance of having upsells in your store.

You don't want to simply make money from your front-end offer; instead, you want to earn the majority of your money through upsells.

In fact, upsells are so important that not having them in place can have a major impact on your store's ability to scale to six figures. Why? Because in dropshipping, front-end items usually only tend to break-even; one sale would only be enough to cover both the cost of ads and the product itself.

For example, on average, your ad spend is roughly 50% of the sale price. So if you sold your item for $10, your ad spend would be $5. But don't forget: you also have to consider the cost of the item, which usually falls between $2-5.

If you didn't upsell a customer to additional items, your profit would be end up being very tiny. But imagine adding a $19.95 upsell to the equation. Can you suddenly see how your profit margins shoot right up?

The best part is, upsells are essentially 'ad free' — you don't have to spend a penny on ads to promote them! And with the profit you earn from this sale, you can use it to scale your store even FASTER.

Think about additional products you can remarket or upsell to your previous customers to get them to buy more. This is what separates 5-figure stores from 6-figure and even 7-figure stores.

Dropshipping Mistake 7: No after-purchase tracking

Customers want to know when they'll receive their order after purchasing from an online store. Yet, far too many new dropshipping businesses assume that their interactions with the customer end the moment they click the "checkout" button.

A lack of communication will hardly reassure your customers about the quality of your business -- instead, they might think your store was a scam!

To provide your customers with peace of mind and avoid complaints, be sure to provide an easy-to-use order tracking system with the assistance of your vendor.

Send email updates when an order is confirmed or shipped. Consistent communication is especially important when shipping delay occurs or if an item is temporarily out of stock. Providing quality service in this regard is key for maintaining customer satisfaction.

Dropshipping Mistake 8: Lackluster returns

One hundred percent customer satisfaction may be the goal, but it's rarely the reality.

In fact, online retail return rates often exceed 30 percent, especially in the clothing industry. If you don't have a streamlined return policy in place, you'll find yourself facing a lot of angry customers.

When selecting a vendor, make sure you set up a streamlined system for handling returns and refunds. Clear instructions and timely responses to customer inquiries (especially in providing a refund or replacement item) will allow you to maintain goodwill with your customers, even when things don't go as planned.

Dropshipping Mistake 9: Only running a single store

Does running a single dropshipping store seem like a lot of work?

The thing is, even if you've done your research and found what seems like a good niche, you never know if your business idea is going to take off until you actually launch your store.

By starting one or two additional stores that are different from your initial niche, you'll be even more invested in your ecommerce career and have a backup in place in case one store flops. Diversifying your risk will protect you from unexpected economic changes and other potential setbacks.

When done right, dropshipping can be a cornerstone of your business model, helping you get orders to your customers in a timely and efficient manner. As you take steps to eliminate routine mistakes from your business model, you'll be able to provide the quality service your customers expect and deserve.

HOW TO PROVIDE EXCEPTIONAL CUSTOMER SUPPORT IN DROPSHIPPING/SATISFYING YOUR CUSTOMERS

Customer service is the role dedicated to helping customers get the value they paid for from a product or service, especially when things go wrong. Many businesses have a dedicated customer service department, but those invested in delivering great experiences make support a company-wide priority.

While great customer service is especially important for businesses that have a strong financial incentive to retain their customers, the bar has risen across all industries, and customers are rewarding businesses that keep pace. This shift has, in turn, evolved support into a revenue driver.

One of the most important touch points you have with a customer is their support experience, so your service must be outstanding.

The support channels you choose determine the level and types of customer service you can provide. The tricky part is deciding where you'll meet your customers and how you'll support them when you get there.

The right support tools help keep your standards high and your response times reasonably low.

It's unrealistic for most small shops to accommodate every possible point of contact that exists today, but it is essential that you choose support channels that fit your business and your customers' needs and commit to a presence there.

Here are a few foundational channels to consider.

1. Email: Provide fast, asynchronous support

Email is easier to manage than live support channels that require you or someone from your team to be available. Email also lets you set reasonable response expectations, which is a substantial benefit for time-strapped entrepreneurs. A note on your contact page can tell customers to expect a response within a few hours, or that email support isn't available on weekends.

Email automatically creates a record of your discussion, easily allowing you to see how satisfied a customer was with their support experience, ask for feedback, and keep track of conversations

A final benefit of email is its simplicity. There are several great tools for managing a fast-paced queue, but if you're a team of one wearing multiple hats, a standard inbox, such as support@yourcompany.com, is all you need to get started.

Tools for email support:

Gmail

Zendesk Support

Help Scout

Gorgias

xSellco

2. Social media: Support your customers in public

Social support differs from other available channels in one fundamental way: replies are public, visible to anyone who wants to see them. Every interaction with a customer over social is a chance to show who you are, and that can make or break a potential relationship with each person who comes across the conversation.

Don't try to be everywhere. Offer customer support on social media platforms where you already have a marketing presence. This should include not only channels you want to spend time on, but also the ones most used by your customers.

Tools for social support:

Buffer Reply

Hootsuite

Sprout Social

Facebook Messenger channel

Build stronger relationships with Shopify Ping

Shopify Ping connects to the messaging apps you already use to bring all your conversations into a single mobile location, making it easier to respond to questions and build relationships with customers—even when you're on the go.

3. Live chat: Fix customer issues in real-time

Live chat is a great way to provide quick, easily accessible support to current and potential customers. As you consider rolling out live chat, think about where you want customers to access it (e.g. high-priority pages on your store) and what you're hoping to accomplish with it.

You may want to invite potential customers who are browsing but haven't finished an order to start a live chat conversation, or enable live chat for customers who have just made a purchase but might have a question or issue.

Tools for live chat support:

Olark

Chatra

Tidio

Re:Amaze

4. Telephone support: Offer a direct line to your business

Many customers still prefer phone calls for urgent, time-sensitive issues, especially if they have a problem with a high-priced product.

Set up a phone line where customers can reach someone directly or leave a voicemail. Small businesses aren't expected to be on call around the clock, so post their availability on your website, along with how quickly customers can expect a voice message to be returned.

Tools for phone support:

Google Voice

YouMail

Aircall

5. Help content: Equip your customers with answers

Head off (and reduce) support questions by creating a Frequently Asked Questions page or other documentation that shares your basic policies and answers the most common queries. Providing your customers with this information, and making it easy to find, gives them the option to self-serve and saves you valuable time.

Every piece of help content you create eventually has to be maintained.

It will take time to know what questions customers are most likely to ask. If you haven't been operating long enough to have "frequent" questions, consider proactively providing answers around these key areas:

Billing

Order processing

Shipping

Returns and exchanges

Your support content should grow and change as your store evolves and adds new products. Revisit your FAQ page on a regular basis and make sure it's up to date.

Tools for help content:

HelpCenter

EasySlide

If you find that a particular customer service channel isn't working for your business, change your availability or sunset it. You want your business to stand out because of the quality of your support conversations and your ability to solve problems as they arise, not because of the number of ways customers can reach you. When you juggle too many channels, you're bound to drop one.

Essential skills to improve your customer service

Customer service sometimes is undervalued due to its reliance on so-called soft skills. That's an outdated point of view. Support has become more technical in recent years, and many of the most important customer service skills don't come naturally to most people, even to entrepreneurs, who frequently act as customer-facing employees in the early days.

It takes time to become great at the distinct and ever-evolving skill set needed for customer service. But no matter what product you sell or where you support your customers, there are a few essential skills that lay the groundwork for all the rest.

1. Know your product inside out

Few things provoke a customer's ire like asking a question and getting a wrong or incomplete answer. It doesn't matter whether you offer an expansive a selection of items, you're dropshipping, or you're new to your product category. Not knowing your products is like a singer forgetting the lyrics to a song onstage.

Both you and your staff need a deep knowledge of what your product is and how it's used. Training new hires, even if they're part-time, should always start with a lesson on what you sell and how it fits into customers' lives.

You can't provide great customer service without being an expert on your product, especially in categories with a knowledgeable customer base, like niche hobbies.

2. Learn to use positive language

Being positive doesn't mean confining yourself to an artificially cheery and upbeat tone. Instead, it's about avoiding negative phrasing that can cause customers to have a negative reaction.

Positive language focuses on solutions, not problems, and gives people a sense of agency. Phrases like "you have to" or "I need you to" might be straightforward and accurate, but can cause customers to feel the burden to solve the problem is on them, even if it wasn't their fault. You can go from negative to positive by making a few simple changes:

Negative: "To start, you'll have to check your order number. OK, thanks. It says here that product won't be available for a few weeks, so I can't place an order for you until it arrives at our warehouse."

Positive: "First, let's verify your order number. Great, thank you! It looks like that product will be available next month. I can place an order for you as soon as it reaches our warehouse."

Customers don't want to be lectured on what you can't do for them, they want to hear what options are available to solve their problem. To keep a customer in your corner, show them you're committed to finding a solution, and use language that invites them to collaborate with you on finding that solution.

3. Adapt your tone to the context

There are two important concepts in business communication: "voice" and "tone." Essentially, voice is the underlying style you want your brand to have, and tone is the appropriate style for a specific context.

A fun-loving dog brand might want to mirror the enthusiasm their customers have for their furry friends. However, responding in that voice without adjusting your tone to an email about a late shipment or a damaged order might come across as grating. Similarly, while your brand's voice generally should be consistent, consider matching the tone of customers who have a different conversational style.

It can be challenging not to abandon your distinct voice for cold corporate speak during a support conversation with a customer who has a problem. Stay consistent and use your brand voice as a foundation while adjusting your tone based the customer's temperament and their reason for contacting you.

4. Crystal-clear writing skills

One of the biggest causes of miscommunication is writing that's clever at the expense of being clear. Creativity is an important part of making a support experience stand out, but your first priority is writing clear, direct answers that can't be misunderstood.

It's easy to assume everyone knows what you know, an unintentional bias known as the curse of knowledge. To avoid this mistake, treat customers as competent, but don't make assumptions about what they know.

Great support starts with writing clear, direct answers that can't be misunderstood.

For example, if you'd like a customer to share their order number, don't just tell them to look for it in their inbox. Provide step-by-step directions on how and where they can find it. Think about the instructions you'd give, and how you'd phrase your response, if you were helping a friend of a friend troubleshoot a problem.

Something else to consider is the way you style your replies, especially over email. Careless styling can cause confusion. Favor easy reading by making liberal use of bullet points, line breaks, and boldface to break up long replies into scannable sections.

5. Advocacy for your customers

Traditionally, businesses are expected to have empathy for their customers. But empathy is only a passive first step in the equation. More important than empathy is advocacy. Advocacy is championing the concerns of your customer and being active in identifying potential solutions. Advocacy works because it's easy to identify and understand—it's felt through action and through descriptions of attempted action.

Customer interactions have three phases:

Sensing: This happens at the start of a conversation, when you ask questions in order to pinpoint what caused the customer's issue.

Seeking: After the problem is identified, you then explore what can feasibly be done to solve that problem.

Settling: Once solutions are surfaced, you can work with the customer to decide on the best outcome.

Advocacy most often occurs during the "seeking" phase. Telling a customer what solutions you've explored can make them even more receptive to a less than perfect outcome. If a customer can see the logic that led you to suggest what you did, they'll be more understanding. If you offer a lackluster solution with no context, they might assume you're trying to brush them off.

The worst thing you can do on a customer service call is appear uncaring. Don't let a placating "We're sorry!" do all the work for you. Take control of the situation, show the customer you're motivated to identify real solutions, and suggest a firm next step or a shortlist of realistic options.

It's important to remember the reason they've reached out for help in the first place is that they've come to a dead end already. They often aren't sure what their options are for moving forward, or how to decide which option is best.

Following up a sincere apology with next steps is key to navigating tough interactions empathetically. First, this approach acknowledges the complexity of their situation and any emotions they may be feeling. Second (and more importantly), it shifts the focus and tone of the conversation back towards addressing the problem at hand. It builds common ground instead of focusing on how frustrating dealing with said problem may be.

6. Creativity to deliver frugal wows

"Frugal wows" are gestures that have no monetary value for a customer, but create lasting loyalty through the gesture's thoughtfulness.

Customers are drawn to things that are free, but free items alone don't necessarily make them loyal. Frugal wows rely on creativity over capital. Here are a few examples:

Sending handwritten thank-you notes

Including creative packaging inserts

Providing samples that complement a purchase

Offering surprise post-purchase discounts

Creating personal connections with short videos

As your business grows, it's good to find ways to deliver repeatable wow moments. Strategically, it's better to delight many customers a little than one customer a lot.

In the quest for efficiency, it's easy to forget that word of mouth isn't gained through neutral experiences. Wow moments shouldn't be the main pillar in your support strategy, but this type of little unexpected extra for your customers still will go a long way in helping build your reputation.

7. Understand how to set the right expectations

Setting the right expectations can directly influence how customers perceive the quality of your support and make the difference in whether they walk away happy or dissatisfied.

Even minor details make a difference: if your chat widget says "Get an answer instantly" and your average response time is actually three minutes, your customers will end up frustrated for reasons you could have avoided.

The golden rule is to under-promise and over-deliver, something that's easier said than done. There will be times when you'll feel internal pressure to make unrealistic promises, like if you're unsure exactly when an item will be back in stock, or if something went wrong with an order and you want to make it up to the customer. Big promises you'll have a hard time living up to, let alone exceeding, can inflate a customer's expectations.

Be especially careful in regards to time. Let customers know at important touch points (such as on your contact page) how quickly they can expect a response. Don't make promises in areas where you can't exercise complete control, like ambitious shipping times.

Why good service improves the customer experience

Customer service needs to be more than a necessary cost of doing business. It needs to create value.

Fortunately, great support provides an open and direct line to your customers, which means it doesn't have to be limited to reactive patching of small issues. Support can result in major improvements to the shopping experience for future customers, and even provide insight on how you can accelerate your business.

1. Effective support solves the root cause

Customer service creates value by surfacing otherwise hidden problems through the unprompted feedback it provides. This can help you prevent issues for future customers by solving the root cause of a problem, rather than simply treating its symptoms.

For example, if you field the same question about a product multiple times a day, you can rewrite that product's description on your webpage, creating a better, more informative experience for future customers—saving yourself the time you were spending responding to that particular question.

Solve the root cause of a customer's issue, don't just treat the resulting symptoms.

This is an example of how efficient customer service can be driven by empathy: you're not looking to avoid customers, you're looking to avoid problems. Customers don't want to contact you about mundane product details. When you use support to prune away problems, you create a better experience for future customers. You'll also likely see a net improvement to your store's buying experience and potentially your overall sales, because you've fixed hurdles that were tripping up shoppers.

Create a simple system to track issues you hear about more than once. If you're not using a dedicated support tool like a help desk, a simple spreadsheet or a Trello board will do.

2. Support can encourage more valuable conversations

Not every customer can be given red carpet treatment during a service interaction; it simply doesn't scale. Without optimizing for efficiency, some customers may have a good experience at the expense of others.

Reality is more chaotic than a 2 x 2 matrix, but this perspective can fundamentally shift how you look at customer service. There's an ideal way for each category of conversation to be handled:

Valuable to you, valuable to customers. If you're helping to close a sale, saving a sale already made, or learning something new from customers, you're extracting a lot of value and want to encourage these types of conversation as often as you can.

Valuable to you, irritable to customers. If customers are annoyed by the hoops you're asking them to jump through, you should lower the barrier by making these steps as easy as possible. Sometimes individual steps can't be eliminated, but they often can be simplified.

Irritable to you, valuable to customers. If the conversation needs to happen but provides zero or negative value to the business, self-service in the form of FAQ pages and help docs can provide customers with the quick answers they need.

Irritable to you, irritable to customers. Do whatever you can to eliminate the source of the problem. No one benefits from these conversations, so consider them a leaky pipe. You can place a bucket to catch the drip temporarily, but, long term, you need to fix the leak.

You might think all is well once a customer gets the solution they asked for. But Price and Jaffe's framework shows it isn't always that simple. Some conversations are indicative of a larger problem, so taking a "ticket closed" approach to supporting your customers will result in a number of missed opportunities.

3. Customer service can provide unexpected insight

Education is at the heart of excellent customer service: education for your customers and education for you. Customers will contact you with questions and issues you'd never be able to surface on your own. Constructive feedback is a gift because it helps you spot opportunities that can potentially shift your entire business.

One important example: customers repeatedly asking you whether you plan to carry a specific product or accessory is a signal that you may want to look into why they're asking and what exactly they're looking for.

Not every customer issue will raise its hand and say, "I'm a problem you need to solve!"

Businesses that don't pay attention to customer behavior and feedback go the way of the dinosaur; just look at the dozens of legacy brands that have fallen by the wayside after a technological shift. Ignoring customers is usually a mindset problem of entrepreneurs thinking they know better. You might be uniquely suited to solve problems, but customers are uniquely suited to share the problems that need solving.

Support is one important way you can keep your finger on the pulse of customer demand and product opportunities. You just need to be willing to listen.

How to handle tricky customer service scenarios

Hearing from upset customers can be one of the most challenging parts of running your own business. It's easy to take their frustrations personally, even if you know there's nothing you could have done differently.

Mistakes are impossible to avoid completely, but the silver lining is that they often provide an opportunity to show your commitment to earning a customer's business. If you can recover from a blunder, your customer might end up more loyal than if the issue had never happened.

When an upset customer contacts you, don't think of it as a missed opportunity to make a good impression, but rather a chance to make amends. Customers want to feel heard and know that you're in their corner to help them reach a positive outcome.

Below are some hands-on strategies you can use to turn a customer's experience around, even when a perfect resolution feels out of reach.

Predict the most likely problems in advance

Some problems will come up more frequently than others. For example, most merchants will be no stranger to customers asking why their order hasn't arrived. It's worth creating a template to address questions like this. Try to identify common questions early on so you're ready for them in busy sales seasons. Once you have a well-constructed response that suits your brand, you can save it as a model for future use.

Know how to close a customer conversation

New entrepreneurs often fumble the end of challenging support conversations by not knowing how to preempt follow-up issues or end in a way that leaves customers feeling heard and appreciated.

Try to empathize with customers by viewing their questions as holistic events: along the way to their original goal, the customer had to stop and ask for help. If you fix their current issue, where are they off to next? What will they have to do? Be able to identify that step and provide help before they ask.

If your support strategy is limited to the "warm fuzzies," you'll end up leaving customers out in the cold.

When it comes to closing a support conversation, think of it as having the right signoff. This is crucial because perception counts for a lot. You want to use language that leaves no doubt you've fully addressed a customer's issue, appreciate the trust they've placed in you, and are open to hearing from them again anytime.

The best language to use when closing a support conversation depends on why a customer contacted you, but here are a few simple examples that show how you can make slight adjustments depending on context.

Customer satisfaction
Many new entrepreneurs begin tracking quality by measuring customer satisfaction (CSAT). Using a number of tools, you can send customers a satisfaction survey at the end of each support interaction, giving them an easy way to share feedback and provide commentary on what they did and didn't like. You can even embed customer satisfaction surveys at the bottom of every email you send.

Keep in mind that most CSAT tools will show your average score. Averages mean very little to the customer who had an especially poor experience, so be sure not to lose sight of personal feedback and anecdotes. Every customer counts. Keep track of low ratings so you can follow up, make things right, and learn from what went wrong.

CSAT is helpful in evaluating customer sentiment, but it's limited to a single moment in time and is fairly broad. It's also difficult with CSAT scores to parse out the real reason for dissatisfaction: it may have been your tone, your policy, or even the product itself. That's why it's important to read the commentary that comes along with your ratings.

"Not everything that counts can be counted, and not everything that can be counted counts."

Customer Effort Score

Customer Effort Score (CES) measures the amount of work a customer felt they had to do to get their issue solved. Customers who have to send several emails, repeat their requests, or search for hours trying to find a solution would report a "high-effort experience."

Tracking reported customer effort and finding ways to reduce hurdles is a growing trend in support. Gartner, which originated the idea of measuring customer effort, has shared data showing 94% of customers with low-effort interactions intend to repurchase, compared to 4% of those experiencing high effort. CES can be revealing because customers want to buy from businesses that provide effortless experiences.

DROPSHIPPING TIPS

Dropshipping is undoubtedly a great business model for any entrepreneur looking to get into ecommerce. It is easy to start, cost effective, low risk, and offers incredible flexibility in terms of time, and what you can do.

Easy as it may sound, drop shipping is a serious business for serious entrepreneurs. New marketers often make common mistakes that see their business taken to the cleaners not long after launching.

There are some things, when done correctly can turn your small store into a recognizable online brand. But, what are these things that new and experience marketers need to pay attention to?

1. Educate Yourself Will Help A Lot

You cannot be good at something if you haven't taken time to learn. If you are to be the best drop shipper there is, you need to really know a lot about the trade.

Some of the most important aspects you have to focus on include the web platform, choice niche, supplier info, and online marketing.

You don't need to acquire deep professional knowledge; a simple yet in-depth research around the topics will help. You'll know where to start, how to go about the venture, and how to handle any problems along the way.

You can obtain a wealth of drop shipping information from Google. There are also online courses about dropshipping on websites like Udemy. Another great place to find dropshipping and online business knowledge is oberlo.com.

2. Know Your Niche More than Your Customers

The first mistake new marketers make is to choose the wrong niche when going into dropshipping. Often, people pick a niche based on what other marketers are saying is going to sell.

Well, not everything sells like hotcake, and those that are in demand have already flooded the market. Prudent sellers go for the niche they are familiar with. Alas, how do you sell a product you are not interested in? Don't be surprised if you find yourself selling to the wrong people!

You'll agree with me that it is necessary that you sell products that you are passionate about as well as those that you have knowledge about.

If you are crazy about children and the environment, but at the same time have no idea what kids crave on different stages, it will certainly help to take a few child psychology and children behavioral pattern courses. Otherwise, you cannot launch a well considered, well targeted kids store.

3. Find the Right Supplier is Extremely Important

It is extremely important that you partner with the right supplier for your online venture. Remember, the supplier will be shipping products ordered from your store directly to your clients.

Imagine the kind of reputation you will get if a supplier keeps sending poor quality products, or fails to deliver on orders. If I order a cashmere scarf and receive a handkerchief instead...well, there's a problem right there.

The only way out is to find the right suppliers you can work with. Here are 3 steps to help you find and keep the right suppliers.

a: Supplier audit. Go through the suppliers' licenses, check their range of products, look at customer reviews, and order yourself a sample.

b: Work with multiple suppliers. Come up with a short list of the best suppliers. Compare product prices, sales services, and guarantees. Work with at least 3 suppliers.

c: Quickly get rid of bad suppliers. Any supplier who sells ordinary watches, but tries to pass them off as genuine Rolexes needs to go.

4. Automate Will Help Save Tons of Time

The good thing about the dropshipping business is that you don't have to be there for every trade done. Once you've set up your store and have laid down a comprehensive marketing plan, you can fully automate everything.

There are quite a number of dropshipping apps and software that handle the automation process. Such automation tools take care of things like inventory management, social media postings, comment replies, targeting emails, AdWord traffic, and so on.

By automating, you free up much time that you can use to run errands or carry on with your 9-5. Even so, there are some things you will have to do individually; SEO, blog content, PPC campaigns etc.

5. Conduct Competitive Intelligence Will Make Your Business Much Easier

The fuss about ecommerce as an easy way of starting a business and making money has created a lot of competition to the point that only the most unique sellers really enjoy the bounty. Competitive intelligence often reveals insightful tricks and tips that your competition is using to get ahead of the game.

Keeping an eye on the competition discloses their strength and weaknesses. This goes a long way to help you become an even better seller.

Plenty of competitor information is publically available and can be obtained through legal means. So, you don't have to peep through office windows nor have their computers hacked.

Here's what you can do to keep tabs on your competition:

- Check their websites
- Visit their social media profiles
- Order their products
- Go to industry trade shows
- Go through competitor customer reviews
- Subscribe to their mailing lists

6. Rev Up Your Customer Service Will Keep Your Customers Coming Back

Customer service is all about conversational commerce. A great customer service is a dropshippers best tool. With a remarkable customer service, you can beat even the giant ecommerce competition in your industry.

Reving up your customer service is all about making the customer feel respected, valued, and important. Don't lure in the customer just to push sales. Rather try to build a solid customer base.

An important thing to note about customer service for dropshippers is that the customers have to see that you actually care for their wants and needs.

Here is how to be a responsible dropshipper who is responsible for their customers' needs.

- Educate
- Communicate
- Build relationships with clients

- Respond to both positive and negative feedback

7. Plan for Returns and Other Issues

Every business faces their share of drawbacks. Some of the issues online store owners will face include back orders, return & refund claims, and lost shipment.

These issues are particularly complicated for dropshippers since there is no direct control over the order processing, packaging, and shipment process. However, these potential problems can be avoided with a proper contingency plan.

You can quickly resolve return claims by having customers send returned items to you. The good thing about receiving returned items yourself is that it gives you greater control and allows you to provide a much better customer service.

The downside of it is the logistics involved; receiving, storage, and reselling.

Fortunately, most suppliers have a return policy in place. If you are going to work with their policy, that means that customers return items directly to the supplier. This takes the work out of organizing for shipping of returns, storage, repair and resale. Even so, this poses the following problems:

• Supplier could reject returned items if not shipped to them in time, or if the item is not in good condition.

• Supplier could charge your customers shipping fee, and restocking fees

• Supplier might have a complex return policy that makes it rather difficult for customers to follow through.

Your obligation as the vendor here, is to discuss the return policy with your supplier and come to an agreement over what needs to be done by who at what point. This will go a long way to help mitigate such kind of scenarios.

8. Test your Product is Extremely Important

As a dropshipper, it is critical that you order a product sample and see exactly what your customers will be getting. Some dubious suppliers send low quality products that may hurt your business.

Your obligation is to your customers. Test your products to know what the products look like and assess whether the customer will be satisfied.

On the plus side, you can use the product samples to take custom images and capture the aspects that your customers want to see. You can also use it for your SEO projects (explainer videos, blogs, etc), and be able to answer customer questions as a "real user".

9. Put Effort into Your Website's Experience

A successful online store owner values customer experience. You have to put effort into creating a web store with a clean interface, easy navigation, quality product images, detailed product description, clear return policies, and a smooth checkout process.

As you optimize your web store for the user ensure also that SEO is clean.

Below are some critical aspect your web store should have:

• About and Contact page

• Professional logo

- Featured product
- Privacy policy
- Return and exchange policies
- Shipping process details
- FAQs page
- Size guide (where applicable)

10. Create Custom Product Images

Being unique sales. Creating custom content sets you apart from the rest of the online sellers. This is a great way to increase traffic to your webstore.

If possible, use your own product images. Capture the different angles that your customers might be interested to view. Using custom product images sets your brand apart because most other sellers are using the same old stock photos.

Make sure you produce quality images and it will up your game.

11. Evaluate Profit Margin Will Earn You Much More

When choosing a product to list on your store, make sure you take a look at its profit margin. Products from different manufacturers sale differently. It is extremely important that the choice product it at a good price point for the service.

Evaluate your choice niche for its product's marketing potential, its competitiveness, and its profit capabilities. The thing to remember here is not to overprice nor underprice your products. Since dropshipping gets you products at wholesale prices, you should be able to set just the right price point – slightly below market value, depending on your competition.

12. Featured Product Will Increase Your Sales

More often than not, your visitors will have decided within the first few minutes whether to buy from you store or move on to the next store- usually, your competition. Within that decisive moment, your customer is usually still on your landing page.

Strategic product placement helps retain the visitor longer on your site. The featured product is strategically placed on the main page of your site so that the customer instantly notices the deal. You must feature popular products, competitive prices, and recognizable discount offers.

13. Focus on Marketing Will Drive You More Traffic

Dropsipping has the one advantage that it is not time, labor, or capital intensive. That means you'll have a lot of time in your hands to take care of things like store optimization, content creation, and marketing – which is in fact where most of your focus should be.

Consider the following marketing channels to drive traffic to your store and maximize success:

• Facebook, Instagram and Twitter Ads

• Google AdWords

• Pinterest Ads

• Email marketing

14. Know Your Customers Than Your Girlfriend

Who are you selling to? Ca you know what they want if you don't know what they need? The most effective marketing strategy is driven by knowledge of the target audience. Collect information about your potential customers: their occupation, earnings, lifestyle, location, their values and interests.

You don't have to follow anyone around or go spying on the social media! Find online communities and forums based around your industry and analyze the group.

Also, try keeping in touch with your customers on social media, direct messages, live chat, and sore comments. By analyzing their reviews, questions, and complaints, you will be able to make better decisions and rise your business.

15. Learn From Mistakes Will Help You Grow Up

Mistakes and failures can teach us some great lessons that potentially lead us to great success in the future. Luckily, these don't all have to be your own mistakes or failure. There are many dropshippers who have come before you, and hundreds of thousands others are still in the industry. There are great lessons to learn from whatever mistakes any of them made.

Below is a collection of the most impactful mistakes that can critically harm your dropshipping business. Carefully research these topics and see where you can improve on to avoid being caught up in the same pool of problems.

- Careless choice of niche

- Complex website structure

- Poor store design

- False discounts

- Incorrect promotion links

- Dubious reviews

- Suspicious number of orders

- Unsupervised social networks accounts

156

IMPORTANCE OF CONVERSION IN DROPSHIPPING

Conversion is key factor you must not neglect, and to increase conversions, there are many factors to consider.

For your online store, conversion is a percent of people who buy on your website in comparison to all your visitors.

The idea to boost conversion rate may be said in simple words "sell more to the same number of visitors."

Better to attract 100 people to your website and sell to 20 of them, than attract 100 people and sell to 5 of them.

The conversion rate is the percentage of visitors who convert— i.e. take the desired action, such as making a purchase from your site or signing up for your newsletter (see Conversion). Conversion rates are calculated by the number of conversions divided by the number of visitors. For example, if you send your email newsletter to 100 people and 42 of them open it, your conversion rate for that particular action is 42%.

How can I raise my conversion rate?

First you should make sure you have a clear idea of whom you are trying to convert and to what action specifically— remember, conversion can mean many things, not just making a sale. In general, the following can help increase all types of conversions:

Clarity. Whether an easy-to-navigate website, a clear call to action, or a well-written email, you'll get more conversions by keeping everything easy to follow and understand.

Good design. This is related to clarity, but also includes the attractiveness of your website, mobile-friendliness, etc.

Authority and trust. If the customer trusts your website and your information, they see you as an authority and are more likely to follow your calls to action. Trust can be built by including accurate information and good site security.

The AIDA strategy. AIDA stands for Awareness, Interest, Desire, Action and represents the states of a conversion in progress. Knowledge of the AIDA model can help you develop your visitors' awareness, capture their interest, give them the desire for your product, and in turn cause them to take action.

What is a good conversion rate?

While an average conversion rate is usually around 2% to 3.5%, a good conversion rate is higher. To determine a good conversion rate, we refer to websites that are in the top 10% of conversions, which have conversion rates of at least 11.45%. Your goal for conversions should always be focused on increasing your rate to match that of the top 10% of websites that have achieved this number.

What's considered a good conversion rate can also vary somewhat by industry, depending on product type, average order value, and where your website visitors come from. For example, an online store selling low-priced products will have a higher conversion rate than one selling expensive products. You can improve your conversion rate through effective use of landing pages and better targeting of your advertising. This approach will ensure that you are

1. Reaching the right customers, and

2. Holding their attention in a way that convinces them to convert (whether you want them to buy, sign up for a newsletter, or take another specific action).

What is conversion rate optimization?

Conversion rate optimization is the process of improving a website so visitors are more likely to convert. There are several aspects to conversion rate optimization, including website layout and other design details like color choice, positioning of calls to action, and adding important (and convincing) information to your page. The technical quality of your website is also important, as a slow-loading or mobile-incompatible website will cause visitors to leave.

Another aspect of conversion rate optimization involves your method of earning traffic for your page, for example, through targeting and wording of your advertisements. Well-targeted ads appear only to customers who would be interested in what you offer, so every ad click is more likely to come from a customer with an inclination to convert. Poorly-targeted ads, however, are shown to people less likely to be interested. The wording of your advertisements comes into play because it controls whether or not a visitor is truly interested in your products or if they end up feeling misled by your ad, at which point they'll leave your site. Ensuring your advertising is well-targeted, and truly representative of what customers will find at your website, are both a part of conversion rate optimization.

HOW TO RETAIN CUSTOMERS

Customer retention is the process of turning one-time buyers into repeat customers.

The word "retention" stems from retain, and retain is basically just a fancy way of saying keep.

So, the goal of customer retention is to keep your existing customers.

The goals and methods of retaining customers vary by industry: A company that sells high-end software will have different customer retention strategies than an ecommerce store.

But for all sectors, the idea is to provide a level of quality and service that keeps people coming back – customer retention perfected.

Let's dive into some of the customer retention strategies that are designed for ecommerce store owners like you.

These customer retention strategies will give your customers the incentive, opportunity, and desire to come back to your store for another purchase.

Set Realistic Expectations

Setting realistic expectations is so important if you're trying to improve your customer retention rate – it can have a huge impact on your business' ability to keep customers.

Think about things like shipping times, for example. Most online stores can't compete with Amazon when it comes to shipping times. But, what you can do instead is work hard to keep your customers informed.

Suppose you have a customer who orders something and then has to wait a few weeks for it to show up. This can go one of two ways:

They have no idea how long shipping will take, and they become increasingly more annoyed every day that their package doesn't arrive.

They knew from the beginning that it would take a little while, so the two-week wait is in line with their expectations, so it's really no problem at all.

If the goal is to retain customers, we want to make sure that we're creating this second scenario.

And there are lots of ways to do it with simple customer retention strategies.

You can have transparent shipping information on your website. You can send emails to customers telling them that their order was received; that their order was processed; and that their item has shipped.

Of course, setting expectations goes way beyond shipping.

Make sure your product descriptions are accurate. Make sure there aren't surprise fees that appear at checkout. Setting clear expectations is a basic, but huge, step forward, and will go a long way when you're trying to improve your customer retention rates.

Create a Loyalty Program

A customer loyalty program is a great way to increase customer retention. These programs reward your customers by giving them incentives to come back and shop with you.

Once your customers opt into your loyalty program, make them feel special by hooking them up with offers: Give them a sneak peek at new products, and offer exclusive deals. This royal treatment will help your customers to feel valued, and is the crux of this customer retention strategy.

You can even give someone loyalty program-esque benefits before they have opted in. For example, you can offer each buyer a discount code inside of their order confirmation email.

Don't make them sign up for anything – just get them the discount straightaway.

If you offer your customers value without any cloaked agendas after they've made a purchase, it'll go a long way to improve customer loyalty and retention.

Pay Attention to Questions

You know how you sometimes need an extra set of eyes to edit because it's impossible to spot your own typos?

The same thing can happen with your store: You designed the customer journey, you built the product pages, you set the prices. In short, you understand everything about your store because you're the one who invented it.

This is exactly why we can't always see what we did wrong. At least not as well as our customers can.

Paying attention to questions about your store is a great way to keep your customers, and a simple customer retention technique.

For example, if someone asks a question that you thought was obvious, that's your clue that maybe it isn't actually so obvious.

Or if they ask a question that you already explained, then maybe you didn't explain it clearly enough or loudly enough.

Make customers feel comfortable enough to ask questions. The more comfortable they feel, the higher your customer retention will be.

Plus, it's like they say – feedback is a gift.

So listen to those questions and remember that if one person is asking it, others might be as well.

And listening is a great way to improve customer retention – if you know what the problems are; you'll have a much better chance to fix them.

Pay Attention to Complaints

The reality is: customer retention depends on customer satisfaction.

If your customers are unhappy with the service that you provide, why would they come back for a second visit?

This means that every complaint you receive is like a mini customer satisfaction survey, so make sure that you use them to improve your customer retention rates.

Essentially, if you get a complaint, don't ignore it.

You could even take steps to make it simpler for customers to submit complaints. Put a Contact page on your website, throw your email into the footer, and make sure that you're available on social media.

Use insights from customer complaints to make the next customer's experience better.

Be Active on Social

If your customers forget about you, you can't retain them. And there are few better ways to stay top of mind than engaging with customers on social media.

If social is going to be part of your customer retention strategy – and it should be! – Then bake it into the customer journey. Put social buttons in your footer, on your checkout page, on your contact page. Everywhere.

When customers compliment your store on social, thank them for the kind words and then share their love with the rest of your followers – this is a great customer retention strategy.

You can also improve your customer retention rates by announcing new products, deals, and other updates on social. That's a great way to generate buzz around your social channels.

You can even put your social buttons in your emails.

Target Customers on Social

Social media can help with customer retention by letting you target past buyers. With Facebook and Instagram, for instance, you can create target audiences based on pages that customers visited – like, say, a "Thank you" page after making a purchase – or on certain events.

When it comes to customer acquisition, so much of the targeting that online store owners do on Facebook is guesswork, at least initially.

They're educated guesses though, at least, which are based on locations, or age groups, or interests, or gender.

But when you use social media to target past customers, it removes the guesswork.

You know the people on the receiving end of these ads made purchases on your site, making social targeting a valuable tool for your customer retention strategy.

Use Email

Each email you send can aid customer retention — even when you're sending emails that aren't really about retaining customers.

Every email can be part of that process. The order confirmation, the shipment-sent confirmation, the follow-up thank you.

These are great opportunities that you can use to set expectations, engage customers, and increase your customer retention rate.

Once you compile an email list, you can use segmentation. For example, you could create segments based on the specific products that customers purchased, how much they spent, whether they used a discount code, and so on.

It seems like email is becoming less popular, at least among certain demographics. But that's not necessarily a bad thing for your customer retention strategy.

As personal communication keeps moving to iMessage, Facebook Messenger, Snapchat, and WhatsApp, emails might become less intrusive: They won't be competing for real estate with messages from friends and family. That means your emails will have a higher chance of helping you hit your goals.

That means your emails will have a higher chance of helping you hit your goals, and if they're done right you'll be able to improve customer loyalty and retention.

Market to Your Customer's Interests

Whenever we talk about customer retention, one thing is clear – your marketing materials must be aligned with your customer's interests.

Why?

Well, if you're looking to improve your customer retention rate, you're not going to do that by sending your existing customers emails which have nothing to do with the things which initially drew them to your business.

Or, if you're thinking about trying out some new content on your social media channels, it's important that you assess why your followers liked your content in the first place. Is the new content that you want to post going to jeopardize that existing relationship?

These are risks which you may need to take on your entrepreneurial journey, but make sure that they're calculated risks. When it comes to customer retention strategies, sticking with what your customers know, not what you know is generally a good policy to stick with.

Engage in Social Responsibility

High customer retention rates hinge on your buyers feeling good – not only about the products that they've purchased from you, but also with the full shopping experience.

That includes price, quality, communication, and so on.

But you can also make customers feel good by letting them know that they are doing good. This is where social responsibility can have an impact.

Social responsibility refers to activities that help people in need. And lots of online stores do a brilliant job of incorporating social responsibility into their business – and letting customers know about it.

Examples include donating a certain percentage of every sale to a charity, or providing a meal for needy children for every purchase.

Talk about building customer loyalty while increasing your retention – if you're seen as a brand that's doing good for the world, it's a lot easier for your customers to back you.

After all, when your customers know that every item they buy will help a good cause; you're giving them an incentive that goes way beyond reliable shipping.

Be Honest

Be honest. It's as simple as that.

It might sound a little vague at first, but there are a lot of people out there who have been burned by businesses before.

Whether that is through faulty products, confusing returns policies, unknown charges, or something else, people are quick to lose trust nowadays.

So make sure that you provide your customers with an honest experience when they're shopping from you.

Offer fair prices for your products and for your shipping rates. Be clear with which shipping company you're going to use and remember to add your tracking numbers.

Don't try to bump your prices too high initially. Nothing will make your customers skeptical more than an unwarranted high price tag.

All in all, try to treat your customers how you want to be treated – this is one of the best ways to improve customer retention rates for businesses of all shapes and sizes.

MOST COMMON DROP SHIPPING PROBLEMS

Getting started with a drop shipping business can be quite challenging. The learning curve can be quite steep with a number of important things to learn. Inevitably, you will encounter some problems either with your drop shipping supplier, or the product that you will need to address to keep your customers happy. Here are some common drop shipping problems and how to get around them:

Selling Items You Have Never Seen Before

One of the quirks about running a dropship business is that you will sometimes be dealing in products that you have never seen in person! This can obviously be a challenge because it's never easy selling something that you have no clue about. Luckily for you, there are a number of ways in which you can get around this problem:

Sell Well-Established Products: Selling products by well-established Dropshipping manufacturers gives you some assurance that your customers will get good quality products. Top manufactures usually have high quality websites with loads of product information including product descriptions, their pictures, and their uses. You can usually learn a lot about new products that you have never seen before by gleaning information from your manufacturer's website.

Order Popular Products for Yourself: If you have several new products that are popular with your customers and you therefore have to ship them frequently, it's usually a good idea to order for samples of these products from your suppliers for yourself so that you can get an opportunity to see them and learn more about them firsthand. If they are expensive or valuable items, you can later resell the items as 'slightly used' or 'refurbished' products on sites such as eBay or Amazon and recoup a good chunk of your investment.

Talk with Your Customers: You can learn a great deal about the products you are selling by talking to your customers. Just call some of your customers, preferably the regular ones, and ask them about their experiences about using your products. This way, you also get to learn more about your customers as well.

Drop Shipping Fraud

One of the common problems encountered with drop shipping businesses and other online businesses is credit card fraud. Whereas the mention of credit card fraud often conjures up images of some sophisticated cyber criminals outwitting your credit card providers' security systems, the truth is that the vast majority of credit card fraud is opportunistic and occurs when you fail to observe some simple security measures.

Protect your drop shipping store from fraud. If you use your eCommerce website as your payment gateway, make sure that you request your customers to enter their CVV numbers – these are the last 3 digits on the back of all credit cards. Entering the CVV number is a good way to ensure that the one making the purchase actually possesses the physical card. Make sure that the gateway service that you use for processing your card is AVS-enabled. AVS, or Address Verification Service, is a security feature that ensures the billing address provided by the customer matches their post code that is on file with their bank. If the two fail to match, the transaction is blocked.

It's always a good idea to keep an eye on large orders if they happen to have a different billing and shipping address because most online shopping cases occur here. If you happen to ship any order to a customer's billing address, make sure that the shipment address matches the customer's bank information.

Having your products drop shipped to addresses that are different from the official billing addresses exposes you to higher risk because if the order turns out to be a fraudulent one, you will be responsible for refunding the genuine card holder for any losses incurred. That's why it's important to be extra careful with such orders.

Always be on the lookout for large orders, email addresses that fail to match the customer's name and orders that come with requests for expedited shipping. In most cases, a quick phone call is usually enough to determine whether an order is legitimate or fraudulent.

High Competition & Low Margins

The unfortunate fact about a drop shipping business is that many products that can be easily drop shipped often spawn a lot of competition. This kind of competition usually leads to cutthroat pricing and thin margins, which make it difficult to build a viable business.

To be successful in such kinds of situations, avoid trying to compete on high value dropship products price alone but instead focus on offering added value to your customers through great product education, selection and service. It's also important to learn about how to spot a profitable niche that is likely to make you more profits.

Also it makes good sense to become a member of a good reliable Drop Ship Supplier Directory that offers metrics that show you potential profits that can be made using historical data.

Syncing Products With Drop Ship Suppliers

One of the problems encountered by new ecommerce businesses that use drop shippers in their supply chain is that sometimes products may become unavailable. This problem has been somewhat addressed by tools such as plugins that use API data to pull information from your suppliers website and update it on your site.

Select the Right Dropship Products. Unfortunately, this method of running a business is bad practice. If you are looking at creating a website and have it quickly filled with inventory through some instant import plugins, you also face the problem of ending up with duplicate content. This simply means, that you have listed a product which has the same word for word description as potentially others that have also used this means to populate their site.

By doing this, you are flagging your website with Google as low quality (as its content is largely duplicated from other sites) and it is inevitable that the consequences will be detrimental. Some of those results in your website being delisted from the Google index altogether, or at the very least, being listed at the very bottom of the search index, requiring you to be funding hefty search marketing campaigns that are simply not viable on a drop ship store margins.

Dealing With Drop Ship Supplier Mistakes

Depending on the quality of supplier you have, the frequency of mistakes in delivered products can be anywhere from quite frequently to very rarely. One sign of a mediocre supplier is one who repeatedly gaffs in fulfillment errors and logistical problems. A good rule of thumb is to always be ready to accept responsibility for your suppliers' mistakes. Trying to pin any delivery problems on your suppliers to your customers comes off as amateurish and in bad taste. Just accept the cost of remedying any logistical problems as part of the business. If a supplier consistently makes such mistakes, make a point of looking for a higher quality one.

A lot of the problems encountered by the average drop shipping reliant business have to do with the supply side of the business. That is why you have to really do your homework when searching for a supplier. Once you have found a good and reliable supplier, make sure you work on your eCommerce website since this is often the first point of contact between your customers and your business. If you manage your drop shipping business correctly, it can form a good foundation for a successful online store.

Conclusion

The only person who can stop you from actualizing your dreams and maximizing your potentials is you. Never stop believing in your self and the things you can accomplish, trust me it's never too late to start and you're never a failure if you fail but you become one if and only if you stop trying. It's never too late to become that independent person you've always wanted to be.

Believe in yourself, you can do it !!!

As you will have understood, it took many hours of work to make this guide. For this reason, I ask you only a favor in return. I would be really happy if you write a positive review on the content of this ebook and give it a 5-star rating. I would really appreciate it.